22.80

Alamance Community College
Library
P. O. Box 8000
Graham, NC 27253

Early Escapades

Early Escapades

by Eudora Welty

Edited by Patti Carr Black

UNIVERSITY PRESS OF MISSISSIPPI JACKSON

Publication is made possible in part by a grant
from the Hiatt-Ingram Fund of the
Community Foundation of Greater Jackson

www.upress.state.ms.us

The University Press of Mississippi is a member of the Association of American University Presses.

All photographs are used with the permission of Mary Alice Welty White and Elizabeth Welty Thompson, Eudora Welty LLC. From the Eudora Welty House Collection and the Eudora Welty Collection, Mississippi Department of Archives and History.

Printed in Canada

First edition 2005

Library of Congress Cataloging-in-Publication Data
Welty, Eudora, 1909-
Early escapades / by Eudora Welty ; edited by Patti Carr Black.
p. cm.
ISBN 1-57806-774-X (cloth : alk. paper)
I. Black, Patti Carr. II. Title.
PS3545.E6A6 2005
811'.52--dc22
2005003967
British Library Cataloging-in-Publication Data available

Acknowledgments

My deep appreciation to Mary Alice White and Elizabeth Thompson for permission to reprint Eudora Welty's words and images and for making available photographs from the family's collection. My thanks to Miss Welty's long-time agent, Tim Seldes.

Special thanks to Jane and Wood Hiatt for their support and sponsorship of the book.

Several people assisted by lending items and granting permissions for use in this compilation. My thanks to Louis Lyell, Reb McMichael, Suzanne Marrs, Pearl McHaney, Fred Smith, Hunter Cole, and Rebecca Moreton. For the assistance given me in using various archival collections, I thank the staff of the Mississippi Department of Archives and History, especially Amy Steadman, Alison Beard, and Forrest Galey; at the University of Mississippi's Special Collections, Jennifer Ford; and at Mississippi University for Women, Gail Gunter and her staff. I would like to acknowledge the help afforded by Steve Pieschel and students at Mississippi University for Women in a summer research project,1983, that identified Eudora's contributions to the W publications.

—Patti Carr Black

Comic Energy

Eudora Welty's Young Art

Patti Carr Black

In *One Writer's Beginnings*, Eudora Welty speculated that her comedic sense surfaced when she was three: "I can't think I had much of a sense of humor as long as I remained the only child. When my brother Edward came along after I was three, we both became comics, making each other laugh. We set each other off, as we did for life, from the minute he learned to talk." Perhaps it was the give-and-take of conversation. Ask anyone who ever had the fortune to be friends with Eudora, or to be given an interview, or to have a one-time conversation or the slightest meeting: the heart of her personality was an open alertness, a lightning-fast intelligence, and, most dazzling, an ironic and brilliant wit. She had an infectious sense of the absurd, which she frequently put to use in her conversation.

The thing many friends remember most is laughter, her own and the laughter she elicited. In her piece "That Bright Face Is Laughing," she wrote that "a sense of the absurd is the most congenial tie in the world." Reynolds Price shared "her sense of hilarity," to Willie Morris she was "quite simply the funniest person I have ever known," and for her long-time friend Charlotte Capers "there was no one finer for fun and games." For everyone there are the books—the writing—where her immense comic energies are concentrated on deep human issues: the ambiguity of relationships, complex struggles for power, the duality of perceptions, fierce commentary on the way we lead our lives. In story after story—"Why I Live at the P.O.," "Petrified Man," "Lily Daw and the Three Ladies," "Moon Lake," *The Robber Bridegroom*—she created laughter around the painful conditions of being human. "I can't seem to resist," she once said. "There's even some humor in *The Optimist's Daughter*, to do with a funeral—which is probably going too far. But life is that way" (Wheatley, transcript of interviews). This book presents her earliest published writing, almost all of the writings done in fun. Reading the pieces and looking at her droll cartoons, we can—much like studying the big bang theory of the universe—feel the comic energy that swirled through her adult writing, and see the beginnings of her satiric force.

When Eudora Welty was eleven she wrote and produced a small book to amuse her brother Edward, who was ill. "The Glorious Apology" is the rollicking tale of Fitzhugh Green, son of "the whispering saxophonist, Artimus H. Green," and a clear showing of her sense of hilarity, her satiric outlook, and her interest in parody. Illustrated with clips she cut from magazines and newspapers, the project put to good use the comic energy that would fuel Welty's life and writing. "Hear What the Critics Say About It!" her manufactured blurb proclaimed, and a manufactured critic came back with a laconic "Haven't read it."

Certain books of her childhood and adolescence were catalysts for her sense of the double edge of comedy and tragedy. She read nursery rhymes, folk tales, French fairy tales, Norse and Greek myths and legends, Edward Lear, Mark Twain, Jonathan Swift, Lewis Carroll, and the fairy tales of the Brothers Grimm (the basis for *The Robber Bridegroom*). All of her life she was attuned to great comedic genius of stage and film. Charlie Chaplin, Bea Lillie, Ed Wynn, the Marx Brothers, Bert Lahr, and, later, Danny Kaye and Bill Irwin were some of her favorites.

From early in Eudora's young life she considered herself a writer. She proved it even before she entered the eighth grade at Jackson High School in the fall of the year 1921. In August, at age twelve, she won a twenty-five-dollar prize for a poem through the Jackie Mackie Jingles Contest sponsored by the Mackie Pine Oil Company of Covington, Louisiana.

Eudora had started her creative career, however, at the age of ten with artwork. A pen-and-ink drawing titled *Heading for August* was reproduced in *St. Nicholas* magazine in August of 1920. At age fourteen she published her first poem, "Once Upon a Time," in *St. Nicholas*, an illustrated magazine for children that had been popular and influential in America for decades. Many other writers also saw their work in print for the first time there: Edna St. Vincent Millay,

St. Nicholas, August 1920

Bennett Cerf, Cornelia Otis Skinner, Rachel Carson, and Ring Lardner, among others. Eudora published "In the Twilight" in *St. Nicholas* in 1925. The poem is conventionally literary rather than humorous, and in it Eudora introduced her vivid use of simile: a cypress tree "casts delicate shadows like old Spanish lace," and the poem dwelled on a subject that always captured Welty—"the moon ruling supreme."

In the summer of 1924 she went by train with her father and his Lamar Life Insurance agents and their wives on a trip to California. Two special Pullmans were chartered for the group of forty-five people going by way of New Orleans, Juarez, Mexico, and the Grand Canyon to reach Los Angeles for the annual convention of national life underwriters. After seeing sights in Los Angeles (including Venice Beach), they returned home by visiting San Francisco, Reno, Salt Lake City, Colorado Springs, and the top of Pike's Peak. A sou-

To the Golden Gate and Back Again, souvenir booklet published by Christian Welty, illustrated by Eudora Welty, 1924

venir booklet entitled *To the Golden Gate and Back Again* was published by Mr. Welty upon their return. It featured six comic illustrations by Eudora. The text, probably written by Christian Welty, gave details of the trip. Other participants on the trip were invited to write their memories in letters published as a supplement, *As Told by Others*. Fourteen-year-old Eudora is the most likely to have penned the letter ostensibly posted from Podunk, Mississippi, and signed Punk Clabberneck. It was a clumsy attempt to write as an uneducated rural man, and one that she later seemed pained to discuss. A lesson learned, perhaps, was conveyed to her great-niece when Eudora told her some seventy years later, "You don't write how people speak by spelling words funny. You write it by listening to the rhythm of the words themselves" (White, "Eudora").

It was Jackson High School that opened a new and broad avenue of publication for Eudora. Her high school days were compressed when the school board decided in 1922 to add a twelfth grade. The students with the highest averages were allowed each year to take an extra course, and after three years were pronounced seniors, which catapulted Eudora forward to graduate at age sixteen in the spring of 1925. Before that event, in her three years of high school, Eudora contributed poetry, short fiction and nonfiction pieces, and pen-and-ink drawings to *The Quadruplane,* the school annual, and the school paper, *Jackson Hi-Life*. Her first work published in *The Quadruplane* appeared in 1922, her freshman year. An illustrated poem entitled "Then and Now" contrasted a stern nineteenth-century schoolroom "taught to the

"The Children's Page," *Commercial Appeal,* Memphis, 1925

tune of a hick'ry stick" to the "wit and clever fun" of her school. The austere school that she drew seemed to come from her mother's reminiscences of teaching in a West Virginia mountain school: cold winters, the ground "white with snow," the log schoolhouse on "a sloping hill." Her next poem, "The Freshie," was written as a parody of the nursery rhyme "Where did you come from, baby dear?" At the same time that she was contributing to her school publications, she was submitting illustrations to "The Children's Page" of the Memphis *Commercial Appeal*. At least five pen-and-ink sketches were published there from 1923 to 1925, and during that period she created a cover illustration for the sheet music of "Mosquito" by Flo Field Hampton, her senior English teacher, who admired Eudora's talents.

In addition to her writing and illustrating, Eudora, like many high school students, had a full schedule. She was on the basketball team, was secretary of the Dramatic Club, appeared in plays, was literary editor of the *Jackson Hi-Life*, and, in addition, maintained an A average. Outside of school, she read voraciously, stayed busy with her crowd of friends, and took art and piano lessons. Family activities included church services, picnics and morning swims, community events like Chautauqua programs, the state fair and election night downtown, and short and long vacations. A famously faithful moviegoer in childhood, she said in *One Writer's Beginnings* that "my sense of making fictional comedy undoubtedly caught its first spark from the antic pantomime of the silent screen, and from having a kindred soul [Edward] to laugh with." As a teenager Eudora began learning photography from her father, who taught her to do darkroom work. She would later put her comic energy into staged photographs of herself and friends and, still later, into taking serious photographs around the state and during her travels.

Eudora's writing quickly grew more sophisticated. For the 1924 *Quadruplane* during her junior year, she wrote a spoof of herself entitled "The Conference Condemns Caroline," which tells of a tired student who dozes off during her studies because she spends so much time and energy on extracurricular activities. She is visited by several figures representing Latin, physics, literature, geometry, and civics, who seem to be Cicero, Archimedes, Touchstone, Euclid, and a contemporary southern legislator. They came as a committee to warn her that when one waits too late to study, all subjects get harder. It's gentle, self-deprecating humor would later be replaced by a fiercer take on the world.

Right from the start, Eudora was making use of the comic elements she admired all of her life: word play, irony, satire, parody, and classical allusions. For the 1925 *Quadruplane*, Eudora wrote "The Origin of Shorthand," in which she imagines Cubedites, a star reporter for the Parthenon Press, going to the Forum in Rome to hear Cicero speak. Fearful of being spotted as a Greek, he wears a Roman toga borrowed from Cicero's "head butler," and carries "several sheets of blank parchment under his arm and a similar expression on his face." Worried about being seen writing in the Greek language, for he did not know Latin, Cubedites on the spot invents the first shorthand in the world.

A new building was being constructed in 1925 to serve as Jackson's junior and senior high school, and Eudora, in anthropomorphizing the buildings, evaluated the attributes of each. In a piece called "Youth and Age" she imagined a conversation between the two: "I am the New Building—the Building of Hope—of Ambition—of the Future. It listens for the Old Building to reply, but the Old Faithful is lost in its Shadows, its Memories, and its Past—and is silent." The words chosen for the new building seemed to be paraphrases of her father, who, according to *One Writer's Beginnings*, "saw life in terms of the future." This was the year Christian Welty's Lamar Life Building, Jackson's first skyscraper, was completed. Eudora characterized her father as a modern man, "his face always deliberately turned toward the future," someone who "loved all instruments that would instruct and fascinate." He would later fit her out with her first typewriter, a red Royal portable.

A crossword puzzle that she constructed in 1925 was a combination drawing and piece of comic writing with outrageous clues to make words fit around the black spaces that spelled out JHS. The theme of the puzzle was Greeks, one of her favorite sources. For the clue "The Greek who was always ready for Saturday night," the answer was Archimedes. She had pictured him earlier with a bathtub strapped to his back going about demonstrating his weight-of-the-body-immersed-in-liquid principle. The puzzle also played with words, a lifetime passion for Eudora. The clue "You always have to use either this word or emu when you need one ending in U" was answered "Gnu." "What a breeze always did in the language of a poet?" "Wafted." And of course, there was slapstick. To her clue "First four words of a popular Greek song," her answer was "Yes, we have no."

Other distractions in high school were described years later by Eudora in remarks at the retirement of Nash Burger, a Jackson friend who with Eudora's help became book editor of the *New York Times*. "High school gave us the chance to see what Nash could do with writing. In English class, he varied the monotony furnished by the rest of us by writing his book reports on imaginary books by imaginary authors. For the school paper, the *Jackson Hi-Life*, and the annual, he would come out with some fine parody—of boys' books, westerns, sentimental novels of the day . . . I remember the Junior Jupiter Juvenile Detective Agency which took up a page in our annual. Nash was its founder and the president."

Eudora in this speech failed to say what she was up to, but "Blinking Buzzards," for which she sent out illustrated invitations, was an imaginary organization of her creation. A classmate received this notice:

> Dearest Mary Ellen,
>
> Fair one, prithee hark unto what I have to say unto thee. Upon this day there hath been organized a new club, "Blinking Buzzards," by appellation, and tis my plea that thee becometh a member. For thou hast a lean and hungry look, which be the motto of the club. Needless to say, I be the organizer. Prithee answer. Eudora, Chief Buzzard. (Larche Collection)

Eudora was a founding member of the Girgil Club, whose motto was "Listen, cram, and be careful for eighth period you may read." The club's colors were black and blue, and the club book was *The Aeneid*. The Girgil Club was "formed by the senior girls who ate lunch at the 6th period. The purpose was to read the Virgil lesson (bad, bad girls)" apparently at the last minute (Larche Collection).

At her senior Hi-Y banquet, Eudora participated in *Wild Nell, the Pet of the Plains*, a burlesque, which was followed by a chewing gum contest. In the spring of the year, Eudora played the role of Peggy Woofers in *Three Live Ghosts*, for which the school paper gave her a nod: "Eudora Welty furnished many good laughs." She was also a member of the Yeller Club, whose purpose was to support the school teams with cheers at all games. Each member was obliged to bring one original yell for every game (Larche Collection). Eudora

The Quadruplane, Jackson High School yearbook, 1923

was selected by her classmates as "Demeter" (Most Dependable) and "Irene" (Best All 'Round). She graduated with a 94.12 average and when asked by the *Jackson Hi-Life* what she intended to be, she already knew the answer: "author."

In those short three years in high school, Eudora contributed over twenty pen-and-ink drawings to *The Quadruplane*. The earliest, in 1923, depicted tiny gnomes romping with gusto on and through a half-opened book. In her senior year she was the major illustrator, with over a dozen drawings. In her own copy of her senior annual, she wrote "Wonderful—Amazing—Unique. The only one of its kind in creation, May, 1925."

Eudora had studied painting and drawing throughout her younger years. The Jackson artist Marie Hull was one of her early instructors, and Eudora would continue to take art courses when she went to colleges in Mississippi and Wisconsin. In later years she admitted that she had wanted to be a painter and thought that she might be. After art courses at

The Quadruplane, Jackson High School yearbook, 1923

the University of Wisconsin, she realized that she "didn't have what it takes." Nevertheless, critics have noted the strong visual aesthetics of Eudora's writing, citing stories "comparable to abstract tableaux with the spatial components of painting, drama and dance" (Weston, "American Folk Art").

In addition to writing for school publications and submitting work to *St. Nicholas* and the *Commercial Appeal,* other exciting things were happening during her senior year. When her father began the construction of the Lamar Life Building, he hired the same architectural firm to design a new family residence which he began building on Pinehurst Street in a suburb on the outskirts of town. Even before the house was ready for occupancy, Eudora's mother invited Eudora's Sunday school class for a May graduation "garden party" on the newly prepared grounds of the property (Larche Collection). In the summer, the family took a month-long trip, vacationing on Trout Lake, Wisconsin, meeting Grandpa Welty in Chicago, taking him to his home in Ohio, then driving to West Virginia to visit the Andrews family, Chestina Welty's relatives (Marrs, *Eudora Welty*). Back home, no sooner had Eudora moved into her new house than it was time to go off to dormitory life at Mississippi State College for Women, two hundred miles north in Columbus.

On campus she quickly garnered a reputation for her verve and creativity. Two months after she arrived, she was mentioned in the November 14, 1925, edition of the college newspaper, *The Spectator*:

> I defy anyone, "Ladies Home Journal," Billy and William included, to be more alive or more in evidence on this particular stamping ground of the flowers of Mississippi than Eudora Welty. I stand back in amazement at the things that woman does. Anybody want posters drawn? Page Eudora—she'll dash you off an exceedingly effective one in no time at all. Somebody to collect annual money? Eudora will do it. Something clever and funny for the "Spec"? That's the best thing she does. Someone for the Dramatic Club Play? Why, faith an' begorra, here's Eudora again—absolutely perfect as wheezing, sneezing, pleasing Miss Trimble in "The Rector." But wonder of wonders—the honor that pleases this freshman the most is none of these—it is that she has the greatest chest expansion in school.

Almost upon her arrival on campus she sought out the same creative avenues she had enjoyed in high school. She submitted to the college newspaper a witty parody on the

The Spectator, Mississippi State College for Women, February 12, 1927

fairy tale of Rapunzel, a poem entitled "Burlesque Ballad." It was immediately published in *The Spectator* in September 1925; in October she was elected freshman staff representative of *Meh Lady*, the school annual; in November she was cast in a play produced by the Dramatic Club and she began writing other pieces for *The Spectator*. In *One Writer's Beginnings*, she wrote:

> I became a wit and humorist of the parochial kind, and the amount I was able to show off in print must have been a great comfort to me. (I saw *The Bat* and wrote "The Gnat," laid in MSCW. The Gnat assumes the disguise of our gym uniform—navy blue serge one-piece with pleated bloomers reaching below the knee, and white tennis shoes—and enters through the College Library, after hours; our librarian starts screaming

> at his opening line, "Beulah Culbertson, I have come for those fines." I'd been a devoted reader of S. J. Perelman, Corey Ford, and other humorists who appeared in *Judge* magazine, and I'd imagined that with these as a springboard, I could swim.

In the November 14, 1925, issue of *The Spectator*, a long comic piece entitled "The Great Pinnington Solves the Mystery" was published. It was submitted by "a Mear Freshman, with three illustrations by the Arthur, and initialed W." For all of its adolescent sheen, its playfulness is irrepressible. Eudora at age sixteen simultaneously wrote a spoof on the process of writing and a spoof on the genre of mysteries. It is a story within a story, within a story, where the author mixes her thoughts as a writer with the narrative itself, with generous asides to the reader. It is as improbable and funny a muddle as a plot by the Marx Brothers, whom Eudora greatly admired and enjoyed.

Within five months of arriving on campus she became a member of *The Spectator* staff. Her reportorial style ran to such items as "The Freshman class meeting was characterized by the Freshmen being kept in the dark both as to the electric lights and the purpose of the meeting." Her first official art offering was a political cartoon chiding the Mississippi legislature for lack of funding. As in high school, Eudora wrote and contributed poetry to the college newspaper. The first poem published in *The Spectator* her freshman year (November 28, 1925) was a masterful spoof of James Whitcomb Riley entitled "Autumn's Here" ("There's a dusky, husky, musky, smoky smelling in the air").

In the second semester of her freshman year, Eudora sang in the spring minstrel show, acted in the freshman class play, and was reelected as the class's *Meh Lady* representative. During her sophomore year she was appointed fire drill captain of Hastings Hall, which greatly amused her; she also portrayed a member of the faculty in a burlesque, wrote the parody titled "The Gnat," appeared in the fall play *IceBound*, portrayed "Ignorance" in a pageant, and was one of thirty-five sophomores selected to serve on a new campus commission (the selection was based on scholarship, personality, and student government record). She worked hard on the staff of *Meh Lady*. *The Spectator* noted that Eudora Welty "has much of the humor of the situation [*Meh Lady* content] in her hands" and that she would also be taking photographs for the annual.

Through all of this activity, her major extracurricula interests were writing and drawing cartoons. In her sophomore year Eudora and a group of friends founded a comic magazine titled *Oh, Lady.* Eudora was listed as a member of the art staff, but she also contributed a comic poem, "Fairy Crepe," as well as illustrations and cartoons. The magazine lasted only three issues. When its founders left school, it folded. In 1927 Eudora also did a cover drawing for *Hoi-Polloi,* a college literary magazine that her friend Nash Burger hoped to publish at Millsaps College.

Eudora's exuberance and delight in writing spoof material resulted one night in a letter to the Hershey candy company. Egged on by friends studying late, she explained to the company's president that she and her classmates, in a poor col-

Oh, Lady, Mississippi State College for Women, 1927

lege in Mississippi, were often hungry. Would the company consider their request for nourishment in the form of chocolates? In a few weeks, a large case of Hershey chocolate bars arrived. Although Eudora and her friends were triumphant and delighted, Eudora's mother was not amused on learning that Eudora had written to the chairman of the board of the Hershey corporation that she was hungry. As an April Fool's joke in the spring of her sophomore year, the year of raging floods in Mississippi, Eudora wrote a bit of pulp fiction, a terse "society" item, and an editorial:

> Misses Frances Davis, Lois Prophet, Katie Davidson, Frances Motlow, Thomasine Josephine Burnadetta, Kathleen Cady, Dana Davis, Eudora Welty, May Risher, and Earline Agatha Robinson were drowned Thursday evening while boating on the Tombigbee . . . Everyone expresses regret that these promising young women should meet so untimely a death.

Eudora's mock editorial "by officials" about the mock news was entitled "Attitudes."

The deplorable death of the nine unfortunates who met their untimely end in the waters of the Tombigbee has caused much comment. Public opinion has greatly censured the seemingly unfeeling attitude assumed by the officials who take this opportunity to justify themselves. There is nothing in the "Handbook" that bears upon drowning, but it has always been our policy to discourage such procedures.

Our position much resembles that of King John in the immortal elegy by A. A. Milne in which James James Morrison Morrison Weatherby George Dupree's mother went to the end of the town without consulting him.

James James
Morrison's mother
Hasn't been heard of since.
King John
Said he was sorry,
So did the Queen and the Prince.
King John
(Somebody told me)
Said to a man he knew:
"If people go down to the end of the town,
Well, what can *anyone* do?"

A mock front-page story headlined "H. L. Mencken Observes MSCW for Next Book" was another April Fool's feature of *The Spectator*. In *One Writer's Beginnings*, Eudora relates that she was later told by Birney Imes, editor of the

Columbus Dispatch, that the issue of *The Spectator* caught the eye of H. L. Mencken, acerbic editor of *The American Mercury*, who mentioned Eudora's editorial in his column as "sample thinking from the Bible Belt."

After two years at MSCW, Eudora was eager for new worlds to conquer. She was accepted by Randolph-Macon Woman's College in Lynchburg, Virginia, and made arrangements to go there. When she arrived she found that Randolph-Macon was not willing to accept her MSCW credits. She quickly changed her plans and enrolled at the University of Wisconsin, in part because her father admired its president and his theories of education and in part because one of her college friends from Mobile, who planned to be a doctor, was already at Wisconsin with an apartment. Frances Winona Davis, nicknamed Dana, was as lively as Eudora. *The Spectator*, in nominating Davis, a senior, for the campus Hall of Fame in 1927, had noted, "We think she has just about the best sense of humor on the campus . . . She is able to collaborate with Eudora in producing a giggle from *Spectator* readers." The two adventurous and witty girls shared the apartment in Madison, but within a short time Dana Davis left Wisconsin, and Eudora was on her own.

The exuberance and vitality so apparent at MSCW seemed dampened at Wisconsin. Years later she wrote to Diarmuid Russell, her agent, about her time in Madison: "I was very timid and shy, younger than the rest and those people up there seemed to me like sticks of flint, that lived in the icy world. I am afraid of flintiness . . . I used to be in a kind of wandering daze, I would wander down to Chicago

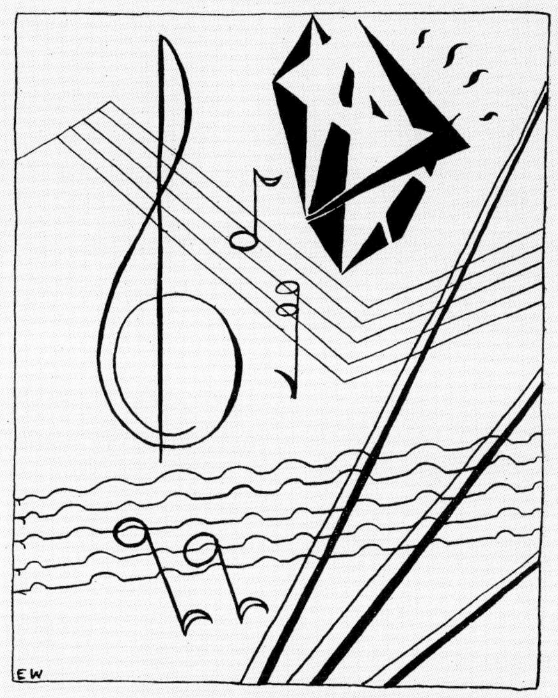

H. L. MENCKEN SINGING THE STAR SPANGLED BANNER IN HIS MORNING TUB

The rapture expressed in the picture on your left is something new in the field of art. Never before has the canvas depicted such spasmodic delight. Note the tremors of patriotism in the upper right hand corner; and close your eyes and see if you can forget. The intense emotion of this composition promises to be unusually alarming to the contemporaries of the artist.

Oh, Lady, Mississippi State College for Women, 1927

and through the stores, I could feel such a heavy heart inside me . . ." (Marrs, *Eudora Welty*).

One might call it loneliness, but she made new friends in Wisconsin, including Felicia White, granddaughter of architect Stanford White, and Pete Dorsett and Migs Schemmerhorn, who later visited with Eudora. Another Wisconsin friend took Eudora to spend Christmas holidays in Montana, where she worked on the small town newspaper published by her friend's father. The daughter of Eudora's landlady provided her with bathtub gin, which tasted to Eudora like "Fitch's Dandruff Remover Shampoo" (Marrs, *Eudora Welty*). While at Wisconsin Eudora wrote a murder story set in Paris, later describing it as "silly" (Nostrandt, "Fiction as Event").The opening sentence, given in *One Writer's Beginnings*, was memorable: "Monsieur Boule inserted a delicate dagger into Mademoiselle's left side and departed with a poised immediacy." The only work by Eudora published at the University of Wisconsin was "Shadows," in the April 1928 issue of *Wisconsin Literary Magazine*. This poem seemed to end her youthful infatuation with writing serious poetry. Over a half century later she had a conversation about poetry with Louis Rubin:

Rubin: Eudora, did you ever write poetry?
Eudora: No.
Rubin: Not at all, not even as a young girl?
Welty: Well, I wrote some in high school, but not since I've grown up.
Rubin: It's a lot harder to deal with the texture of everyday

experience, to document the world around you, in poetry than it is in prose, don't you think?

Shelby Foote: I don't think anything's harder than prose.

Eudora: I don't, either.

(Rubin, Jr., "Growing Up in the Deep South")

In any case, her creative energies were focused on prose—fiction and nonfiction—for the rest of her career. ("A Flock of Guinea Hens Seen from a Car," a poem written by Eudora when she was an adult, was published in *The New Yorker*, April 20, 1957, and privately printed by Albondocani Press in 1970.) Late in life, asked when she became aware of a desire to write, she responded, "I was a big reader, and I sort of thought in terms of imagination and words. It was natural, I think, to want to write. But it's an entirely different matter to be a serious writer. I don't know when that began—I guess after I went to college at the University of Wisconsin. There were some good professors in writing and in literature who made me feel that I was in touch with something" (Ferris, "Interview").

While at Wisconsin, Eudora read voluminously, visited Chicago occasionally, and kept up with her class work, which included art courses. Her thesis at Wisconsin, a novel entitled "All Available Brocade," has never been located. It may be some early, untitled story among her unpublished papers, or perhaps Eudora destroyed it after getting a disappointing and uncustomary B as her grade on it.

After receiving her B.A. degree in English, Eudora returned home in the spring of 1929. Locating work was hard enough for a young woman without secretarial skills, and by fall the Wall Street crash obviated even the possibility of doing so. She began writing occasional pieces for the *Jackson Daily News*. Unlike straight society items or news coverage, these pieces were alternately insightful, absurd, and satiric essays on such topics as a weekly baby clinic for underprivileged children and a history of vacationing. In her essay "Language of Flowers," Eudora uses her extensive knowledge of gardening to create a masterful send-up of both etiquette and the reader. By using historical and straightforward information from an etiquette book concerned with the language of flowers, she draws the unsuspecting reader slowly into the piece. Suddenly the reader is jolted by the advice that "with London Pride, a Lobelia, and some Laburnum," one can say "your frivolity and malevolence will cause you to be forsaken by all." Later in the romp, she writes, "The expression of flowers is varied by changing their position. Place a marigold on the head, says the etiquette book, and it signifies mental anguish; on the bosom indifference."

Even a piece about the serious business of the Jackson Junior Auxiliary, an organization to which she belonged, takes a satiric turn. Assigned to do a public relations piece on the league-sponsored baby clinic, she cannot resist an aside. In her description of the waiting room Eudora has a baby say, "You others may be underfed, all right, but I, after all, am under-privileged." A piece on summer vacations traced the history of vacationing from the prehistoric era, when women did not go with their cavemen mates on vacations ("No man is going to drag a woman 40 miles"), to the

The Mountain Goat, University of the South, February 1932

modern era ("In this day and time one is practically required to go to Yellowstone and fry an egg in a geyser"). She noted that vacationing is a part of our civilization, else "where would people put all that ointment?" She also submitted pen-and-ink drawings to *The Mountain Goat*, the University of the South's student magazine which Nash Burger was then editing.

During the year at home she made plans with five of her high school classmates to attend graduate school at Columbia University in New York. Leone Shotwell Ricketts described the genesis of the idea: "In the summer of 1930, I telephoned Eudora and said, 'If you will go to Columbia University with me, Aunt Mary will let me go.' She took about one minute and said, 'All right'" (Ricketts, "Distinguished Dame"). Eudora had been enamoured of New York since her first visit with her father; she pictured herself in Manhattan going to theatre and museums, and, on the side, working so that she could write fiction. Her father feared that, with a major in English, she would never find employment and urged her to take courses at the Columbia Business School. In the fall of 1930, Leone Shotwell, Mary Frances Horne, Aimee Shands, Joe Skinner, Frank Lyell, and Eudora arrived at Columbia University. The girls were required to live in Johnson Hall, Columbia's graduate dormitory for women under twenty-one, but Eudora set about sampling the many treats that New York had to offer. She was enchanted with vaudeville and went as often as possible to the famous Palace Theatre. She said, "I was the only college student who went to Broadway at ten o'clock on Saturday mornings and didn't emerge all day. I went every week, never missed a change of the bill." Decades later she could quote entire Bea Lillie lyrics, vividly describe the moves of W. C. Fields and deliver Bert Lahr and Ed Wynn punch lines. The advertising course that she took was not of great interest to her, certainly not as much as the offerings of Manhattan. She and her friends went often to the theatre, to museums, art galleries, nightclubs in Harlem and Greenwich Village, even to night court. Eudora later told her great-niece that she and her friends would sneak into speakeasies, drink needle beer and look for gangsters (White, "Eudora"). Serious writing took a backseat.

Living in Johnson Hall under the tyrannical eye of Miss Eliza Rhees Butler turned out to be a comic adventure. Miss Butler was the sister of Nicholas Murray Butler, Columbia's president, and a formidable woman. Extremely condescending to southerners, she put them in their own wing of the dormitory, explaining that southern accents might annoy the other girls. The ever-watchful Miss Butler counseled the girls that they must never accept an aspirin from a stranger or they might become victims of the white slave traffic in New York and "wake up in Buenos Aires in a house of prostitution." Amused, Welty sent off for buttons that she and her friends wore, identifying themselves as WST, "White Slave Traffic."

Butler denied the southern girls free opera tickets that she had been given to distribute, explaining that they were not sophisticated enough to enjoy opera. Eudora and her friends went to the opera nevertheless and were delighted one evening to hear a familiar but offended voice boom out just before the curtain went up: "I am Eliza Rhees Butler,and I have been seated behind a *post*." They watched the opera in high glee and satisfaction with their good seats. As for Eliza Rhees Butler's appearance, Eudora penned a poem that paints a fully realized portrait:

> Where'er she goes forever more,
> The Butler bosom goes before.
> But still and all, I think you'll find
> That most of Butler goes behind.

Eudora's roommate, Aimee Shands from Jackson, was studying for a degree in psychology under Sigmund Freud's famous associate, Alfred Adler. Aimee was unenthusiastic about Adler's suggestion for her master's thesis, which was to take a five-year-old boy to the lion's cage at the zoo and study fright. As Eudora reported, Aimee didn't know a five-year-old boy in Manhattan and decided that she needed a subject closer at hand. She chose Eudora. Every night that Eudora went out for an evening on the town and arrived back at the dormitory exhausted and ready for bed, Aimee presented her with a long questionnaire that she had devised for her new thesis topic, fatigue. Occasionally Eudora went to lectures endorsed by Aimee. She and Jackson friend Frank Lyell attended a night class to hear Professor Hollingsworth, a world-renowned authority in abnormal psychology; Eudora doodled and made notes as she listened (Welty, notes on lecture).

In the summer of 1931, Welty had the excitement of landing her first job in Manhattan and seeing her advertising copy in print. The job proved to be a scam and led to great disillusionment on Eudora's part. The employer was an advertising agency which routinely used college students as interns whom they dismissed after a two-week trial period. In this way the agency kept their workforce going during the Depression without having to ever pay a salary.

Eudora was called home shortly after that debacle, in the fall of 1931. Her father was seriously ill with leukemia and died shortly after her return. In 1929 he had founded WJDX, the first radio station in Jackson and the first in the state to be affiliated with a network, NBC. After Mr. Welty's death, station manager Wiley Harris offered Eudora a part-time job at WJDX. She was given the responsibility of starting a

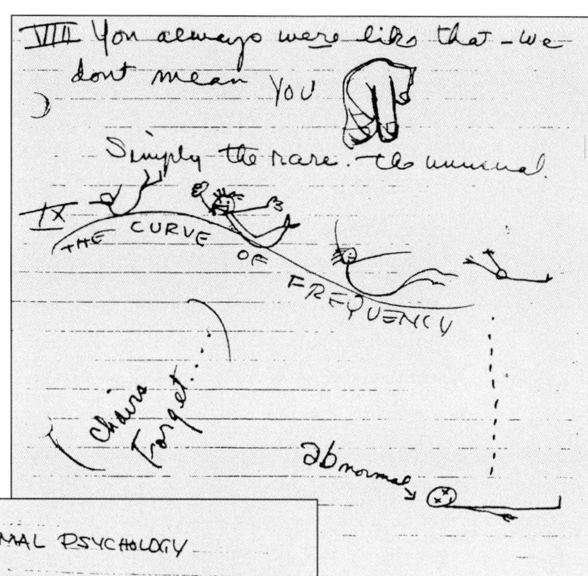

Notes from abnormal psychology lecture, Columbia University, 1930. Used by permission of Louis Lyell.

weekly newsletter for the community, listing the station's plethora of programs—music, theatre, news, feature stories, and profiles of artists. She was the entire staff, compiling the schedule of the shows, writing feature articles and previews of shows, selecting interesting fillers, and penning her own column, "The Editor's Mike." The newsletter was a perfect forum for Eudora's word play, wit, wide-ranging interests, and satiric writing. Her comic energy seemed to be in full swing during her two years at the studio atop the Lamar Life Building. She kept the WJDX staff amused and on their toes, occasionally writing a column alternately entitled "About the Studio" or "Studio Chatter." She wrote: "We wanted to make up limericks for everybody in the studio, but it's too hard. There is, for instance, Duke Rybnick, whose name wouldn't go in a lybnick, though he plays on the cello like a very good fellow, that mustachioed romeo, Rybnick."

She started a chain reaction, with other people on the staff attempting verse. In the September 18–24, 1932, issue of the *Lamar Life Radio News* she wrote: "Notice to the person or persons who wrote a poem in these columns saying it was impossible to write a poem about me: many other than you have discovered this. It's not just the hot weather. It's something fundamental. The one way I could help you out would be in moving to Flora, Miss., but I don't want to. This is just to let you know I understand. I've tried writing poems about me myself. I simply don't rhyme."

She unabashedly admitted that part of her job was writing fan letters to the station. Eudora explained that it was in a good cause: "Dear WJDX, I *love* getting the opera on Saturday. Don't ever take it away" (Ferris, "Interview"). In another "Studio Chatter," her rundown of staff activities included the following: "Miss Eudora Welty is fitting up a pent house in a gully in her back yard, in which she can privately edit the Radio News and chew gum." It seems likely that she may have intended to use the little house that her brothers had built to work on serious fiction, which she began in earnest to write that year.

Still interested in living in New York, Eudora made two trips there during her WJDX tenure. In the spring of 1932 she was in Manhattan for three weeks, and in 1933 she spent three months job hunting in New York. She applied for a job with *The New Yorker,* sending an audacious letter of inquiry in the style, according to Suzanne Marrs, of one of their most popular writers, S. J. Perelman. Her ploy failed and she applied to the *National Geographic* magazine, then for a secretarial job (Marrs, *Eudora Welty*). Nothing materialized in those depressed years. She stayed a while longer at WJDX, worked briefly as a photographer for a dress shop and for the Jackson chapter of Junior Auxiliary, and later did occasional substitute teaching, a profession that she felt incapable of pursuing, as she noted in *One Writer's Beginnings*: "I lacked the instructing turn of mind, the selflessness, the patience for teaching, and I had the unreasoning feeling that I'd be trapped." She wrote briefly for the short-lived *Jackson State Tribune*, contributing a long tribute to her friend, Lehman Engel, a successful composer in Manhattan. Her mother took in a boarder and began giving bridge lessons to supplement their income.

From the fall of 1933 to 1935, Eudora wrote society pieces for the Memphis *Commercial Appeal*. Needing the job, she took her assignment seriously. Most of the "society" families were in her circle of friends and she herself attended as a guest many of the parties and events she covered. Nonetheless, her satiric eye was barely fettered in her descriptions, as in this one from the September 10, 1933, edition: "Speaking of feathers, no bride has worn them yet, although they all read in Vogue that they could do it. However, the next best thing—a maid of honor wore the color chartreuse . . . as far as we know—the first time it's been in a wedding. That is a mark of advance we consider." (The chartreuse gown was worn by Bethany Swearingen, a friend of Eudora's.)

She seemed to try to discipline herself for straight reporting of the social goings-on in Jackson, but she wrote with barely disguised flippancy about weddings, debutante parties, Mardi Gras balls, fraternity parties, bridge and tea parties, horse shows, and travel by "the smart set." Her eye for detail and her knowledge of the structure and strictures of society would mark her later fiction. Knowledge of gardening came in handy with descriptions of weddings where the bridesmaids "carried huge arm bouquets of pink briar cliff roses. The maid of honor carried beautiful Joan Hills." The genre of society writing, she knew, had its own potential for comedy. One of her favorite practitioners of that discipline was the serious Mrs. Beatrice Boyette, who wrote for the *Jackson Daily News*. Eudora saved a typed copy of one of her favorite Boyette columns and labeled it "by Beatrice Boyette and her thesaurus." An excerpt:

> Splendor emitted atmospheric radiance, as the bride was predominant in white lace sparsed with linen, matching accessories and carnation corsage . . . The living and dining rooms, redundant with lustrous spring flowers, diffused essence of felicitousness as the bride made incision in the wedding cake, reposing on an incomparable hand-crocheted table cloth.

Eudora's zest and exuberance kept life in Jackson fun. She had many friends, including some from high school, and the artist Helen Jay Lotterhos, who took her on sketching trips. Her literary friends—writers Hubert Creekmore, Nash Burger, Frank Lyell, Seta Alexander (a witty raconteur), and Lehman Engel, on his trips home from New York—amused themselves by posing for outrageous photographs, gathering for lively conversation, music, and drink, going on picnics and road trips, and taking in the movies and jazz concerts at the Alamo Theatre, where she heard Bessie Smith, "a beautiful woman in an apricot satin dress" (Wheatley, "Eudora Welty"). The group called themselves the Night-Blooming Cereus Club, their motto being "Don't take it cereus, Life's too mysterious." Literature was often a subject of discussion and satire. They played a variety of word games that they invented, including Who Were You With?, the Movie and Wine Test, Dullest Remarks, Cliches, and a favorite that Eudora invented, Old Magazines, in which they wrote dialogue balloons for photographs (Marrs, *Eudora Welty*). They also enjoyed well-known word games like Tom Swifties and a sketching game called Heads and Tails, in which one person drew a body and folded the paper and the next person drew a head. Eudora wrote Frank Lyell in 1933 that she had devised a game called Mississippi Murderers and Cannibals. Eudora's love of games endured her entire life. In 1942 she would write Katherine Anne Porter: "I miss you so much and hope some day again we can just sit down and play a little spit-in-the-ocean with center card and sevens wild and you draw."

Frank Lyell especially shared Eudora's sense of hilarity. When he went to Princeton, their letters to each other offered a lively exchange of puns, parodies, limericks, games, and funny news items. For his long train trip to New Jersey from Jackson, Eudora prepared "a limerick for each stop along the way." For a change of pace she presented him with a couple of rounds of the game Reed Smoot, where one starts with a phrase or word and attempts to arrive at a designated word or phrase through word associations. Starting with "World's Fair," she took this word path to Hawaii: "World's Fair, Fair & warmer, Warmer My Wandering Boy Tonight, Tonight You Belong to Me, Me oh My, My Man, Man Ray, Ray for the Red White & Blue, Blue Heure, Heure Night in June, June Bugs, Bugs Baer, Baer Back, Back to My Little Grass Shack in Kalala Kalne [*sic*] Hawaii. Quite a distance" (Lyell Collection).

During all of this time, after her father's death, Eudora was attempting to do serious writing at home, a process that at first was "secret." She began sending manuscripts to magazines and making photographs with a serious purpose in mind. She had been taking family and travel photographs most of her life, but in 1933 she began "studies of Negroes, with an idea of making a book" (Welty, letter to Abbott). In the collection of photographic negatives that Eudora later donated to the Mississippi Department of Archives and History, many of the 216 taken between 1931 and 1935 were studies of black Mississippians. She had not taken the photographs with any attempt at humor; they were made as documentation of black life in the South. In 1934, when she applied for admission to a photography class in New York taught by Berenice Abbott she explained that she was taking her photographs in response to the photographs (staged and romanticized) by Doris Ullman, which were published as *Roll, Jordan, Roll* in 1933 (Welty, letter to Abbott). When Abbott's class work did not materialize, Eudora went to New York in the fall of 1934 to try to sell her photographs to publishers. A collection of prints offered to Harrison Smith and Robert Haas, Publishers, was rejected because they felt the book would not be profitable (Marrs, *The Welty Collection*). During 1935, she read extensively, wrote constantly and took photographs all around the state. She finished "Acrobats in a Park," a story that would not be published for forty-three years, and "The Children," which she incorporated into her 1942 story "The Landing" (Marrs, *Eudora Welty*). Her first photograph to be published, in June 1935, was titled "Pickup—Deep South," and appeared in *Eyes on the World; A Photographic Record of History-in-the-Making* (it was called "Making a Date" in *One Time, One Place*.)

As 1935 drew to a close, Eudora's life was about to explode with good fortune. The next year would see a story of hers published for the first time. "Death of a Traveling Salesman" came out in *Manuscript* magazine in June 1936. She had her first one-woman photography show in New York at Lugene Opticians Gallery in March 1936, and in the summer she got her first full-time job working in Mississippi for the Works Progress Administration. She later wrote that the WPA work gave her the chance to travel and to see for the first time "the nature of the place" she had been born into. It mattered. In *One Time, One Place*, she wrote, "[W]hen at the age of twenty-one I returned home from the Columbia Graduate School of Business—prepared, I thought, to earn my living—of the ways of life in the world I knew absolutely nothing at all. I didn't even know this. My complete innocence was the last thing I would have suspected of myself. Anyway I was fit to be amazed."

And amazed was how she remained. She has defined a true sense of humor as "human apprehension of other human beings" (Lima, *Eudora Welty Newsletter*). Always curious and unblinking, she saw the world, and without sentimentality she embraced it, with its marvels, its chaos, its mystery. Penetrating beneath the sometimes absurd surface of life with passionate sympathy, she celebrated the inherent value and humanity of the individual.

WORKS CITED

Ferris, William R. "Interview: Eudora Welty." *Southern Cultures* (fall 2003).

Larche, Mary Ellen Wilcox. Senior scrapbook, 1925. In Mary Ellen Wilcox Larche Collection, Special Collections, J. D. Williams Library, University of Mississippi, Oxford, Mississippi.

Lima, Tereza Marques de Oliveira. *Eudora Welty Newsletter* (summer 2000).

Marrs, Suzanne. *The Welty Collection: A Guide to the Eudora Welty Manuscripts and Documents at the Mississippi Department of Archives and History*. Jackson: University Press of Mississippi, 1988.

———. *Eudora Welty: A Biography*. New York: Harcourt, 2005.

Nostrandt, Jeanne Rolfe. "Fiction as Event: An Interview with Eudora Welty." In *More Conversations with Eudora Welty*, edited by Peggy Whitman Prenshaw. Jackson: University Press of Mississippi, 1996.

Ricketts, Leone Shotwell. "Distinguished Dame Eudora Welty." *Tattler* (Jackson, 1973).

Rubin, Louis, D., Jr. "Growing Up in the Deep South: A Conversation with Eudora Welty, Shelby Foote, and Louis D. Rubin, Jr." In *More Conversations with Eudora Welty*, edited by Peggy Whitman Prenshaw. Jackson: University Press of Mississippi, 1996.

Schuster, M. Lincoln, ed. *Eyes on the World; A Photographic Record of History-in-the-Making*. New York: Simon and Schuster, 1935.

Welty, Eudora. Notes on the lecture "Abnormal Psychology" at Columbia University. Enclosed in a letter from New York, Frank Lyell to his family, September 24, 1930. Used with permission of Louis Lyell.

———. *One Time, One Place*. New York: Random House, 1971.

———. "That Bright Face Is Laughing." *The Kenyon Review* 5, no. 2 (spring 1983).

———.*One Writer's Beginnings*. Cambridge: Harvard University Press, 1984.

Weston, Ruth. "American Folk Art, Fine Art, and Eudora Welty." In *Eudora Welty: Eye of the Storyteller*, edited by Dawn Trouard. Kent, Ohio: Kent State University Press, 1989.

Wheatley, Patricia. Uncut transcript of interviews with Eudora Welty for the British Broadcasting Corporation's documentary *A Writer's Beginnings*, 1986.

———. "Eudora Welty: A Writer's Beginnings." In *More Conversations with Eudora Welty*, edited by Peggy Whitman Prenshaw. Jackson: University Press of Mississippi, 1996.

White, Elizabeth Eudora. "Eudora, My Great-Aunt." *Tattler* (Jackson, special issue 2002).

Correspondence

Eudora Welty to Berenice Abbott, August 9, 1934. Quoted with permission of the Welty Estate.

Eudora Welty to Frank Lyell, 1933. In Frank Lyell Collection, Mississippi Department of Archives and History, Jackson, Mississippi.

Eudora Welty to Katherine Anne Porter, summer 1942. In Special Collections, University of Maryland, College Park, Maryland.

1.

What Spell Does This Strange Book *cast over its readers?*

Examine it free for 5 days. If it does not give color, charm and magnetism to your personality, return it within the 5-day period—and the examination will have cost you nothing.

YOU have had books that entertained you—books that interested you—books, even, that amazed you. But never a book like this!

Here is a book that seems to cast a spell over every person who turns its pages!

Almost every page radiates brilliant ideas. Every paragraph guides you unerringly in developing a new, dominant, powerful, magnetic personality.

A copy of this singular book was left lying on a hotel table for a few weeks. Nearly 400 people saw the book—read a few pages—and then *sent for a copy*.

In another case a physician placed a copy on the table in his waiting room. More than 200 of his patients saw the book—read part of it—and then *ordered copies for themselves*.

You *can* sway and control others! You *can* command success. You *can* influence people to do things you want them to do. *This strange magnetic book shows how!*

Once for the Wealthy Only Now Within the Reach of All!

"The Glorious Apology"

By E. Welty

A flaming story of the men who tame rivers of steel—How one of them seared the craven fear from his soul

Your Name in Gol

- on this Wonderfu

for every 10 purchase

The Glorious Apology

A collage book written, designed, and hand-lettered by Eudora, 1921, at age twelve

HEAR WHAT THE CRITICS SAY ABOUT IT!

ANDREW VOLSTEAD— *"Never heard of it."*

WAYNE B. WHEELER— *"I haven't read it."*

JOHN ROACH STRATTON— *"I know nothing about it."*

"—remarkably good!"

H. L. Mencken — *Greater Than the Mona Lisa*

ARTHUR — **"You Must Have Spent *Years* on Shorthand"**

"I Don't Know of a Happier Way to Have Spent My Life"

1.

The Glorious Apology

a tragedy

Chapter I

"Alas!" murmured Fitzhugh Green to the admiring public. "What else is there left in life?"

There was no answer.

Fitzhugh however was unaffected.

It was ever that way.

Chapter II

"Well anyways," pursued Fitzhugh as the prey eluded him, "there is nowhere left to go."

"Oh yes there is," ~~tittered~~ parried Lallie coyly. "Hell."

"Aw go way back and sit down" sniggered Fitzhugh.

Chapter III

"Well," suggested Lallie one night after they had counted their parchesi gains for the evening, "why not go on a GORILLA HUNT?"

"Ha ha thass easy" came back Fitzhugh like a flash. "We have a gorilla."

"Darling" breathed Lallie "What would I do without you?" (see illustration)

Chapter IV

"Well," continued Fitzhugh, "we will leave. You never can tell where these excursions of mine will end," he added, beaming modestly as becomes the son of Artimus H. Green the whispering saxophonist. "I wonder what we will travel in," he mused. "All our cars are being used or worse."

He peered reminiscently out the window. The sight that met his eye caused fond thrills & remembrances.

The sight that met his eye . . .

Chapter V

"Well Lallie," called Fitzhugh from under the house, "look what I got to travel in! Or should I say with?"

"I will be out in a moment, Darling," said Lallie in muffled tones.

She was beginning to be homesick already, and there was a lump in her throat.

But "Gad! This meat is tough!" was all she said.

Look what I got

I will be out in a moment she said in muffled tones..

Chapter VI

Slowly slowly Lallie walked to the door to see what Fitzhugh had got. There was a great weight seemingly on her heart. Leave all this?!!?

There was a great weight . . .

Chapter VII

As she walked down the hall toward the door, Lallie's head was full of fancies: What had Fitzhugh found to travel in? He was very resourceful, she knew. Once he had won $4.98 at eucre.

Her head was full of fancies...

Chapter VIII

At last Lallie reached the door....

Chapter IX

Then? —"Fitzhugh darling!" came Lallie's glad cry. "A nifty little bike! How unusual! Dear, where did you get it?"

"Once It Was an Old Washstand" replie[d]

Fitzy, "but I am sensitive about it. Are [you] about ready to take off? We have only 35 minutes left," he added. "Why don't we get a new clock?"

"Yes I am ready Darling," replied Lallie. "Have you all the supplies?"

"Lorelia," announced Fitzhugh, firmly calling her by her given name, which she had passed on to distant relatives the *next* Christmas you may wager,—"I have decided to dispense with the supplies, as You will take up all the room on the handle bars. I am doing this for your own good."

"Yes Fitzhugh," murmured this little woman preparing to mount the bike.

But suddenly an interruption occurred.

A dainty ankle bared for nought!

'Twas ever thus.

And the interruption? One minute boys while we change the reel.

It was in the form of a delegation from the Weathe Bureau. Fitzhugh quailed visibly.

Chapter X

"See here Green" snarled the leader of the delegation, thrusting a barometer in the young boy's face, "What do you mean by allowing that wife of yours to go out in this garb when the barometer is falling like an omelet!

"I — I didn't mean anything," stammered Fitzhug who had never taken advantage of the numerous 15-min. courses offered for his benefit. "I never mean anything! Will it ~~~ will it kill her?" he asked tremulously.

" She'll never pay this fearful price " declared the other impressively.

"But why— *WHY?!*" shrieked F.

"Heh heh" sneered Delegate Mc Gooflenish ironically. " - perhaps it's *comedones** ".

Chapter XI

Now Lallie appeared again. She had altered her touring costume & gaily ran out to the bike. "How do I look?" she cried sweetly.

"Natty," shouted Fitzhugh, admiration written all over his face, which marre his visage to some slight extent & caus a couple of ink spots to appear on his collar "Now I know you are safe! Hop on!"

And they galloped away.

Delegate Mc Gooflenish laughed up his

How do I look she cried...

sleeve and unfortunately was suffocated; he had to be immediately attended to.

Chapter XII

"Ain't we got fun?" inquired

Fitzhugh, parodying the famous old anthem. "Lallie sweet, you look different."

"You always said I was different," evaded his wife. "But I will confess: I was in disguise a while ago."

Fitzhugh nodded in mute understanding.

"O look at the gorgeous cattails growing by the roadside!" ejaculated Lallie suddenly. "Let me pick some!"

And she scampered down to pick them.

Chapter XIII

But what lay behind them cattails? Alas
Beasts! Feared birds of prey! ~~alas~

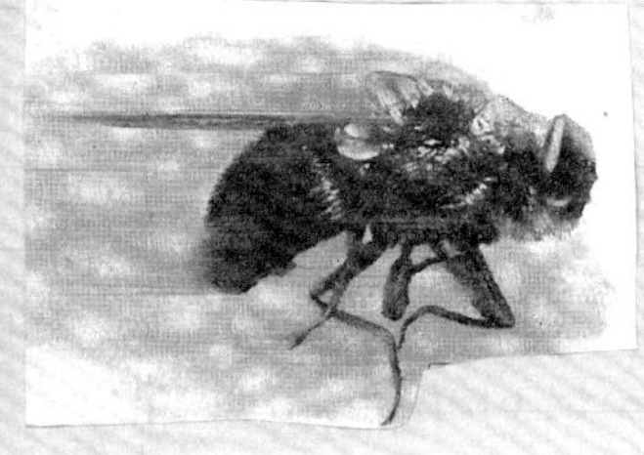

Ten lambs at once are fed with milk by this ingenious feeder, invented by an Iowa sheep raiser. Babies' nursing bottles are used

And O ye fiends! In the midst of them all — LALLIE!
ALL ALONE!
OH FOR THE SOUND
OF A HUMAN VOICE!

Fitzhugh to th' Rescue

"I will get there yet!" he yelled, & kept repeating t himself the cheering words" **Travel For "Uncle Sam"**: Suddenly the wagon broke down. But the horse was still good: leave him in the lurc nay. He mounted the brawny steed and as he cantered fiercely along the jungle pike he could imagine himself on a yak, hunting the *ovis poli* in its bleak Asiatic haunts Suddenly he saw a huge yellow bird named Carolyn snatch Lallie up in her long bill and ~ ~ ~ swallow her! Heavens. He stopped where he was, accosted the bird and told he to do the right thing & quick **Gargling alone is not enough!**" he warned the noisome bird.

At length the poor Lallie was retrieved & forgiven.

tch
tch

"Now we must be on our way," remarked Fitzhugh. We have lost valuable time. Even a little thing like this counts much."

And giving her a fond pat they rode away.

"And here let us say goodbye."
Au revoir!

Then and Now

From *The Quadruplane,* 1922. Poem and illustrations published in the Jackson High School yearbook when Eudora was in the eighth grade.

Then and Now

'Twas the winter of the year;
The ground was white with snow;
The wind was whistling dolefully;
The heavy clouds hung low.
Upon a sloping, smooth worn hill
With foot-paths to and fro,
A little log-built schoolhouse stood,
One hundred years ago.

An old schoolmaster, on the hill
Was ringing to and fro
The worn and rusty iron bell
To call the children, slow.
On up the hill, trudged hand in hand
Two children, Sue and Joe,
Who played and frolicked with the rest,
One hundred years ago.

The small schoolroom held but sixteen
When filled on every row.
The tall desk of the master
Stood on a platform low.
Readin', writin', and 'rithmetic
Were taught by Mr. Know—
Taught to the tune of a hick'ry stick,
One hundred years ago.

65

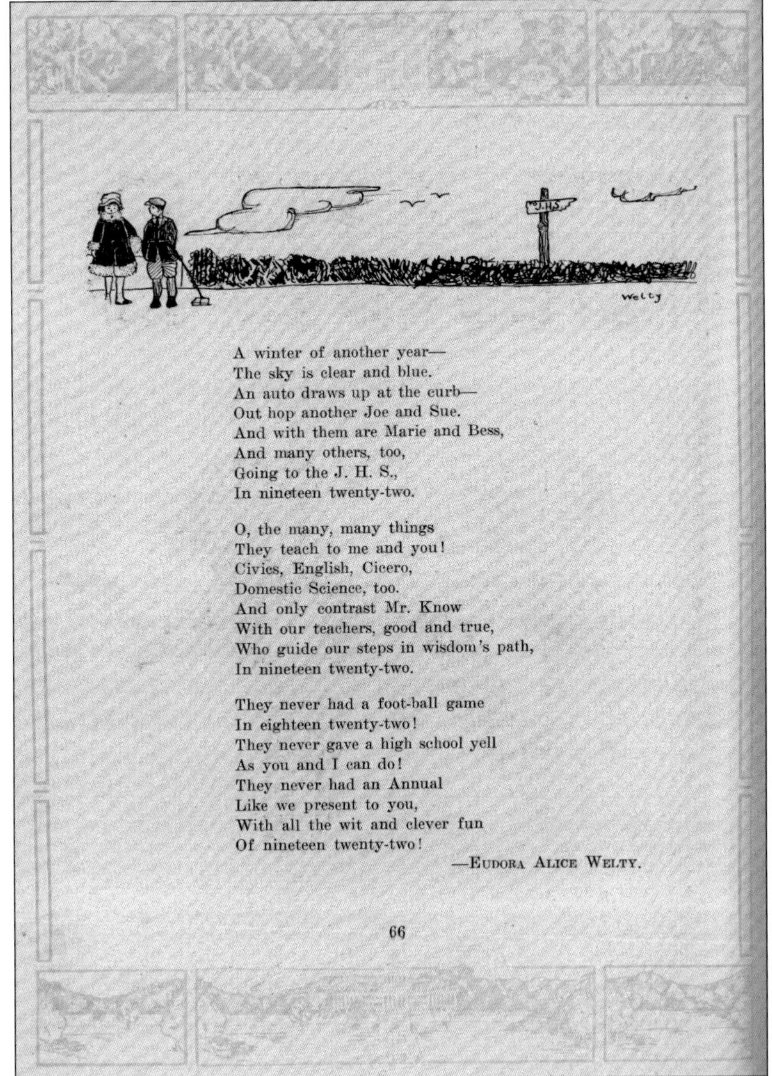

A winter of another year—
The sky is clear and blue.
An auto draws up at the curb—
Out hop another Joe and Sue.
And with them are Marie and Bess,
And many others, too,
Going to the J. H. S.,
In nineteen twenty-two.

O, the many, many things
They teach to me and you!
Civics, English, Cicero,
Domestic Science, too.
And only contrast Mr. Know
With our teachers, good and true,
Who guide our steps in wisdom's path,
In nineteen twenty-two.

They never had a foot-ball game
In eighteen twenty-two!
They never gave a high school yell
As you and I can do!
They never had an Annual
Like we present to you,
With all the wit and clever fun
Of nineteen twenty-two!

—Eudora Alice Welty.

66

The Freshie

From *The Quadruplane*,
Jackson High School, 1922

Where did you come from, Freshie, dear?
Out of the Grammar School into here.

What did you bring with you, my dear?
High hopes and ambitions mixed with fear.

What do you hope to do down here?
Make as good marks as I made last year.

What is your ambition, Freshie, dear?
To head the Honor Roll, every year.

What do you fear, O little one?
I fear the sting of the Sophomores' fun.

Why do you walk with footsteps slow?
I am never sure which way to go.

Why do you wander from place to place?
I'm searching for some familiar face.

Why are you quaking from top to toe?
We might have a test—you never know.

Why do you wear that desperate look?
Father says I must learn to cook.

What thought inspires that flashing eye?
That I'll be a Sophomore by and by.

Yearbook Illustrations

The Quadruplane, Jackson High School, 1923, 1924

The Conference Condemns Caroline

An autobiographical spoof published in *The Quadruplane*, Jackson High School, 1924

The ebony clock on the mantel-piece clanged eleven times, and Caroline sank a little deeper into the soft cushions of the great winged chair and let her book slowly slip from her tired fingers. She would rest just a minute, she thought, before beginning on the next lesson. It seemed only a few moments to Caroline before the quiet of the room was suddenly broken, and accompanied by the rustle and rattle of paper, a diminutive figure stepped, apparently, from between the covers of the "Six Orations" she had been studying. The creature was clothed in a long, cloak-like garment, which hung in voluminous folds from his shoulders and terminated in a border of Roman design about his knees. He looked cautiously about the room for a minute, and then, in low, silver tones, he uttered the single word, "Venite." And an amazing thing happened. There was a slight rustle of pages, and from each book emerged another curious figure. From the Physics book came a little old man, as distinctly Greek as the first one had been Roman, who carried a bath-tub strapped on to his back. Caroline remembered the picture of Archimedes, but, curiously enough, she felt no surprise that it should have suddenly walked out on her study-table. A red and yellow midget jingled his bells and kicked the covers of a small copy of "As You Like It" impatiently as he tumbled out. A fourth figure seemed made of a triangle, whose sides, extended indefinitely in straight lines, formed his legs, and whose circular face smiled good-naturedly. The last member of the group had a long cigar in one corner of his mouth, and he immediately sat down upon his civics book and carelessly elevated his feet upon one another. "Why were you so late in calling us?" he drawled. "When do you think we are going to sleep if you call these committee meetings so late at night?"

There was a mumble from the red-and-yellow figure about the fact that he usually took his rest during committee meetings anyway, but it was not noticed.

"Sleep doesn't worry." It was the old Greek Speaking—"But my experiments and calculations are very important, and cannot be interrupted so late at night."

"O Citizens!" exclaimed the Roman, "who of us do you suppose does not know the reason of this outrage? It is Caroline of the Junior class, Caroline of the Basket Ball Team, Caroline of the Picture-Show Club! It is Caroline, I say, who does everything else before she studies her lessons, and then falls asleep over a masterpiece like my oration against Catiline!" His voice had risen as shrill and high as he could force it, and he was glaring with a terrible eye at Caroline, who, although she wanted to protest vigorously against this denunciation, was sitting awed and spell bound in her chair.

"I have written a message to her," continued the Roman never removing his gaze from the girl. "It read thus: 'How long, O Caro—'" "The gentleman from Rome is out of order," a drawling voice interrupted, and the lanky figure of the Legislator arose slowly to its feet. "I move that the following resolutions be adopted:"

(1)Be it resolved that Caroline should prepare her afore mentioned lessons in the afternoon or early evening, and never again commit the crime of trying to study after ten o'clock at night.

(2)Be it resolved that if said Caroline should violate said

injunction and postpone said study period until late at night, the following penalties shall become increasingly longer and more involved; her figures in geometry shall become more intricate and her theorems more difficult to prove; when she studies late at night, she shall be unable to distinguish between a simile and a metaphor; in her Physics, she—"

Clang! The sound reverberated through the silent room and the startled Caroline rubbed her eyes in amazement. What had happened? Then her gaze fell upon the ebony clock. The hands denoted eleven-thirty. She must have been asleep! She must have dreamed it all! "Anyway," thought Caroline as she gathered up her books, "tomorrow I'm going to study in the afternoon."

In the Twilight

Prize-winning poem published in *St. Nicholas* magazine, 1925

EUDORA WELTY

Jan. 1925, Age 15

Silver Badge

IN THE TWILIGHT

The daylight in glory is dying away;
The last faded colors are fast growing gray;
The sun nears the beckoning portals of night,
And leave to the skies his long, ling'ring light.

The sunbeams have hid 'neath a sad, misty veil,
And softened to shadows—dim, silvery, pale.
The Queen of the Night shyly peeps o'er the hill,
And reigns in her radiance—soft, cold, and still.

A lone cyprus-tree, with its feathery grace,
Casts delicate shadows, like old Spanish lace,
On the cool, trembling waters that meet the gray sky,
And the moon rules supreme in her palace on high.

The Origin of Shorthand

From *The Quadruplane*, Jackson High School, 1925

"Cubedites," quoth the Parthenon Press to his star reporter, "go thou to the Forum in Rome this day, for methinks there is a scoop in store for us. Cicero is to deliver a noble oration against that vile interloper, Catiline."

"But," interrupted Cubedites, "hast not the word reached thy cauliflowers that no fair sons of Greece may hear the oration? Wouldst have thy star reporter hurled into the muddy Tiber ?"

"Aha!" laughed the editor, coyly. "But my noble brain hath conceived a plan. This be it: procure thee a Roman toga; don it, and then thou may'st go in safety to the Forum, where thou can'st take notes in peace and leisure."

"By Jove!" exclaimed Cubedites in admiration. "Thou hast the goods! I shall act in accordance with thy suggestion. Farewell!"

That afternoon, the portly Cubedites, bearing several sheets of blank parchment under his arm and a similar expression on his face, presented himself at the Forum. His Roman toga was not recognized as one borrowed from Cicero's head butler, and he found an advantageous position from which to take notes.

But suddenly a fearful thought occurred to him; even though he were dressed in Roman costume, would not the notes he would take excite suspicion because they were in Greek language. He could not write in Latin. What should he do? What could he do?

While these turbulent thoughts were torturing his mind, Cubedites had nervously twisted the figured hem of his toga into a knot. And as he became aware of this fact and busied himself with the loosening of the knot—came—the—dawn.

A few minutes later, when Cicero came before the people with his oration on his lips, neither he nor any one else realized that his speech was being recorded in the first short hand in the world. But it was a fact, nevertheless, for Cubedites, from the angles and curves on the hem of his toga, had created a script.

Illustrations from *The Quadruplane*

In 1925, her senior year at Jackson High School, Eudora, age sixteen, provided illustrations for the school yearbook.

Divider Page for Sports Section
From *The Quadruplane*, Jackson High School, 1925

Divider Page for the Freshman Class

From *The Quadruplane*, Jackson High School, 1925

Divider Page for the Sophomore Class

From *The Quadruplane*, Jackson High School, 1925

Divider Page for the Junior Class

From *The Quadruplane*, Jackson High School, 1925

Divider Page for the Senior Class

From *The Quadruplane*, Jackson High School, 1925

QUADRUPLANE—'25 J. H. S.

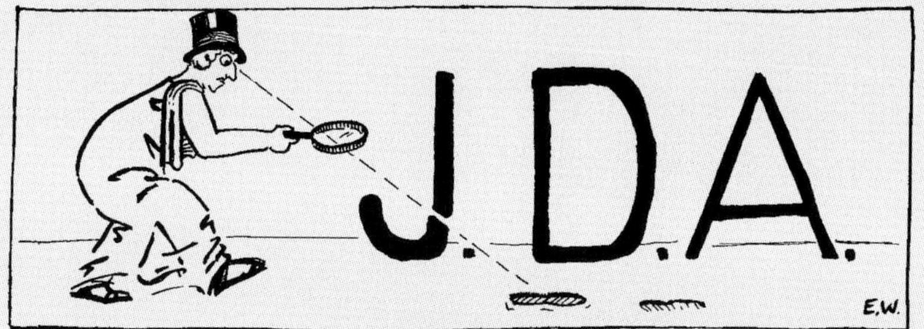

Motto—Non Possumus Officeri.

Purpose—To apprehend Grover Cleveland Bergdoll.

Password—Buttermilk!!

CRIMES COMMITTED or APPREHENDED

—In Business since 1923—

MEMBERS

Herndon Hicks
Calvin Wells
George Stephenson
Buford Yerger
Earl Connerly
Willia P. Wright
Nash Burger

We will catch and convict boot-leggers, burglars, pick-pockets, peanut smugglers, book-borrowers, tablet swipers. Or what have you?

The Junior Jupiter Juvenile Detective Agency was a fictitious club created by Nash Burger.

From *The Quadruplane*, Jackson High School, 1925

The Girgil Club, a lunch club, was created by Eudora and her friends in order to read their Virgil assignments for the next period.

From *The Quadruplane*, Jackson High School, 1925

President.................................Ruth Gainey
Vice-President.................Beth Heidelberg
Secretary........................Dorothy Simmons
Treasurer.............................Willie Sullivan

Motto: Listen, cram, and be careful
For eighth period you may read.
Colors: Black and Blue.
Club Book: The Aeneid.

Members: Beth Enochs, Ruth Gainey, Beth Heidelberg, Mary Flowers Jackson, Annie McNair, Dorothy Simmons, Willie Sullivan, Virginia Vance, and Eudora Welty.

Other yearbook section titles

From *The Quadruplane*, Jackson High School, 1925

Other yearbook section titles

From *The Quadruplane*, Jackson High School, 1925

Crossword puzzle

Created by Eudora for *The Quadruplane*, Jackson High School, 1925

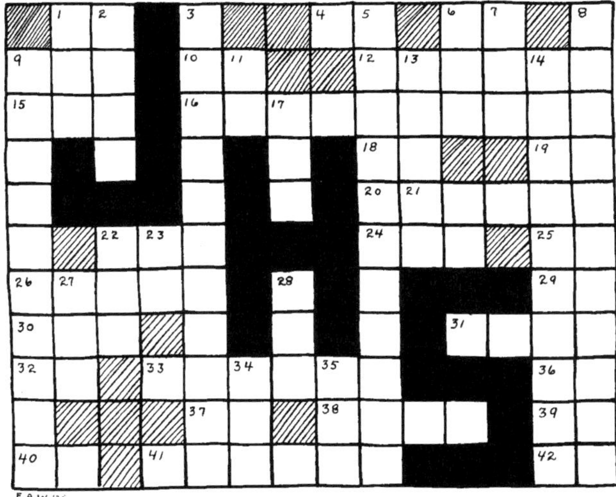

HORIZONTAL

1—Before Exams (abr.).
4—Where Greek aeroplanes go.
6—I hope you know me by this time.
9—Greeks probably use this when they shoot billiards.
10—You and me.
12—They never had a news-paper as good as this in Greece.
15—What the 18th Amendment prevents the Greeks from getting.
16—The Greek who was always ready for Saturday night.
18—What little babies in Greece say.
19—An expression of disgust.
20—To set fire to (this is serious).
22—You always have to use either this word or "Emu" when you need one ending in "u".
24—The thing a Greek hangs his hat on.
25—The initials of one of our business managers.
26—What an Indian (not a Greek) gives when he has a pain.
29—Eating Association (abr.).
30—What a Greek is when the ball beats him to the plate.
31—I have my nerve when I spell it like this.
32—The abbreviation of a Greek railroad.
33—What a breeze always did in the language of the poet.
36—A form of the word "be".
40—A gentle way to say "shut up".
41—The Greek god's Western Union.
42—What the Greeks do when they do something.

VERTICAL

1—If you can't hook something you want, you do this.
2—You spell this with simple ease.
3—The year's best book.
5—A Greek runner we'd like to have on our team.
6—A drink that Greeks like.
7—The thing that Pandora lifted which started all the trouble.
8—First four words of a popular Greek song.
9—We.
11—Sears-Roebuck (abr.).
13—What you see in the mirror.
14—What the Spartan boys would have liked to sleep on.
17—The animal that made whiskers famous.
22—Sometimes used instead of "have".
23—One of the words that makes or mars your life.
27—Little Bennie's last name.
28—Greeks must do this to live.
34—Not against.
35—The female that started all the trouble.

Answers to Crossword Puzzle

HORIZONTAL

1. B. E.
4. Up
6. Al
9. Cue
10. Us
12. Hi-Life
15. Rye
16. Archimedes
18. Da
19. Aw
20. Ignite
22. Gnu
24. Peg
25. H. H.
26. Whoop
29. E. A.
30. Out
31. Nero
32. R. R.
33. Wafted
36. Be
40. Sh.
41. Hermes
42. Do.

VERTICAL

1. Buy
2. EEEE
3. Quadruplane
5. Phidippides
6. Ale
7. Lid
8. Yes, we have no
9. We
11. S. R.
13. Image
14. Featherbed
17. Cat
22. Got
23. No
27. Hur
28. Eat
34. For
35. Eve

Burlesque Ballad

Parody of the fairytale, "Rapunzel," published in *The Spectator*, student newspaper of Mississippi State College for Women, September 26, 1925. Eudora had just arrived as a Freshman.

Up in a tall and silent tower
A maiden labored by the hour,
A nail file back and forth she drew
To saw the window bar in two.

She wept sad tears to show her grief,
And on the ground with dire relief
A pigeon caught them in his bill,
And quenched his thirst with right good will.

And then a knight came riding by
And heard the maiden sob and cry,
He sang a song to cheer her up,
She threw at him her drinking cup.

It struck the knight right in the nose.
It knocked him down and soiled his clothes;
He looked above, he looked below,
And both were pierced by Cupid's bow.

The knight, he sighed in deep despair
How could he reach his lady fair?
No ivy hung upon the wall
And if there did, the knight would fall.

Up in the tower the lady fair
Unbound her coils of golden hair,
She let her locks fly out the casement,
They reached well nigh down to the basement.

Uprose the knight with right good will
And toward his love be climbed with skill;
He bent the bars, and leaped inside,
With out-stretched arms he clasped his bride.

Then to a bar he bound her hair
And carefully lowered his lady fair
He put a lock into his boot
And slid down like a chute-the-chute.

Alack! his spur did cut her head!
Alack! alas! it killed her dead!
The knight was grieved beyond repair
And strangled himself with her golden hair.

The Great Pinnington Solves the Mystery

(By a mear Freshman)
(Illustrated by the Arthur)

From *The Spectator,* in *The Blue Pencil Review* (a supplement), Mississippi State College for Women, November 28, 1925

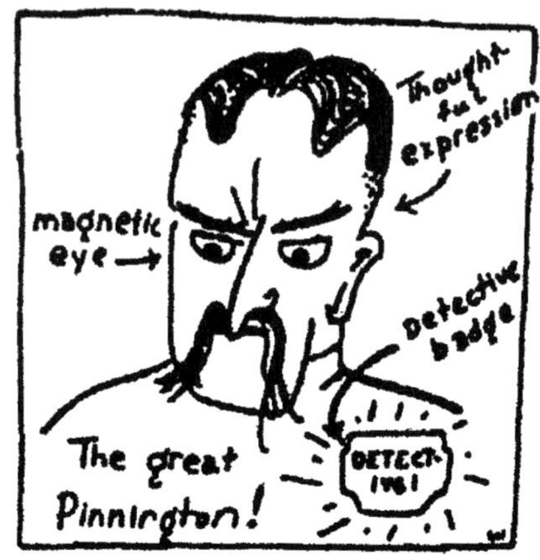

"I am going to be a detective with a magnetic eye."

I am going to write a book. All my friends say that they are confident I can write something big and different, and this is it. Of course, I am not starting in just like that (snap of fingers). Miss Blue, (name disguised) my English teacher, says that to write a book, one has to use one's discretion, and one should never let one's impulse overrun one's knowledge of oneself. I think I will scratch out that sentence, and write it over with the ones changed to yous. No, on second thought, I think I will not, on account of the ones sounding so refined and authorish like. So I have thought for four (4) nights straight about a plot for this book, and so far I have thought of several things. One is, I am going to write it in the 1st person, so that I can be the hero. Of course, since I am in real life a Girl, I should be a Heroine, but a hero is much easier to describe, on account of the fewer number of adjectives you have to use. Maybe I will be the Heroine, too—can't call her "I" of course. But I can endow her with my qualities and characteristics, except that I am not going to let her have big ears like I have. I don't think it is discreteful for a heroine to have big ears, although they look very well on me, people say, because my head is so big back where my cherubim is that my ears look comparatively small.

Another thing I have thought of for this book is that I am going to be a detective with a magnetic eye and a long front name, like Pentington. I would like it to be Pentington, except that somebody else got it for his detective. Notice I didn't say their detective. Another thing Miss Blue told me is not to be trite, so I can't use "Pentington" on account of it being trite. I think I will have Pinnington. I think Pinnington is a noble name. I think that now is the time to start my book. As soon as I kill a fly that is in one of my ears, I will start. All great authors have peculiarities, and mine is that I simply can not write with a fly in my ear.

I have killed the fly. He is on the windowsill.

Now I will start. Miss Blue said all stories should start off with a bang, so I am going to start right anyway. This is the beginning, right the next sentence—

BANG! ! ! !

"What was that?" I muttered in my sleep, as the pistol shot rang out over the quiet house. It was a large house painted green, with white French doors and the cutest light fixtures—all wrought up iron lantern things.

There was no answer. By this time I was fully awake, and, jumping into my Kimona, or whatever it is men wear, I rushed out into the hall. Still I heard no sound except Mr. Jones, the disguised name of the man whose house I was in, who was snoring. But this was not an uncommon noise, because I have found that most men named Jones snore, and anyway it gave me assurance that the man who was murdered wasn't Mr. Jones.

There is another fly bothering me now, but I haven't time to kill him.

So I sped down the hall till I got to the last door on the left hand side, which is the usual place for murders. This was where Mr. Royster was supposedly peacefully sleeping, and yet I felt an odd moment of terror and apprehension, as I stood before the door. Royster is the middle name of a boy I know at school, but that isn't the reason I'm naming the murdered man Royster. I just wanted to.

I knocked on the door. There was no answer, not even snores. My heart stopped beating, but not for long, because you can't live if your heart stops beating for over four seconds. My science teacher said so, and she ought to know, because she went to our state college where I am a Freshman this year, I sure do hate those navy-blue uniforms.

Well, so I tried the door, but it was locked from the inside. I did not know what to do for a minute, but suddenly I remembered. So I did what I thought of, and it opened the door.

After I opened the door, I said "AH!" because the Royster man really had been murdered just as I had thought all the time. He had been shot with a Colt pistol by a man with a hair trigger. I deducted this by looking in the second drawer

"**That fly is here** again. He is a nuisance.'

of a perfectly adorable mahogany vanity dresser and finding this pistol. There was a bullet missing, but I thought I knew where I could find it. I looked—and there it was.

Now, I thought, was the time to break the news to the rest of the family, so I called them together by firing the pistol into the air three (3) times. That brought them together all right. I had thought it would.

At first they seemed inclined to think that I had killed Royster myself, on account of hearing the three shots, etc., but I quickly proved my innocence by showing them that while I had fired three shots, there was only one shot in the body. That fly is here again. He is a nuisance.

Everybody wanted to know who had killed Royster, of course, but I thought I would not tell them yet, because it will come in so handy for the climax. So I told them just to be patient, and to be careful who they loaned two bits to, right then, because, who knew, it might be the murderer who wanted railroad fare, and might probably never return the money.

After I had told the family this, both of them went back to bed. But I slept no more that night. Ah, no. In a minute I am going to cuss that fly out.

I have not written anywhere near a book yet, and I am about to give out of story. So I will have to fill up the extra space with a description, which is the way authors do. I will describe the heroine. I have not mentioned her yet, because I was not absolutely sure I was going to need one, but you see it is always best to think ahead; you never know when you are going to need a heroine or something.

The heroine's name is Josephine. I have named her Josephine so that you can remember she is the heroine on account of both words ending in "ine." I think that it is a good policy, and would advise all authors to follow it so readers could remember which is the heroine by her name, and the hero by his, etc. Of course, nobody had better take Josephine. I thought it up first. But a suggestion for a hero is Nero and any author is welcome to have her hero Nero for nothing, or free gratis, as we say in Latin. Latin always did come easy for me, which I guess is because I am so Literary.

Well, I started out to describe the heroine, but I reckon I got off the track. Sometimes I do, but I always get back in. That is, nearly always.

Josephine was small, but did not look like Gloria Swanson, which would be trite. She had black hair and blue eyes and little feet and a sense of humor. She was forever telling the funniest jokes, and once she won $2.00 on her contribution to Bright Sayings of the Children. She was beautiful and we loved each other dearly. Sometimes I have had to go without a new disguise because of our dear love affair. Disguises cost $16.00, and they are not good disguises at that. (Memo: ask mother how to spell disguise.) Folks get used to them. Especially the disguise with the blind man's tin cup and blue spectacles and sign to hang around the neck. I think that sentence is a clever personal touch.

That fly is giving me a personal touch now. That sentence is a pun. Or at least something like one. I know it is one of those funny things. I am going to kill the fly. I did. He is on the windowsill. That makes 2 on the windowsill.

The next morning I called the family together to explain the mystery to them. They were both rather awed by my explanation and were inclined to dispute it at first, but when I showed them the bloodstained handkerchief and the finger prints, why of course they were bound to accept it.

The next day I had the criminal arrested and put in the jail down behind the court house. We are going to build a new court house next January.

After I had put the criminal in jail, I went back to the house and married Josephine, who is the heroine. Oh yes, I said that before. We are now living very happily together and yesterday was our wedding anniversary, so I went down to town and bought my wife the most adorable negligee you ever saw—all lavender with dawn-colored flowers embroidered on the front, and it's a precious fit.

Josephine gave me some cuff buttons. Or maybe you call them lynx. They were a very nice fit also.

That is all of my book, I think. Of course I will have to go back over it and put in a detail or two which I have overlooked, but for the most part, it is finished. That word "detail" is pronounced with the accent on the tail. You have to be very careful about pronouncing words right when you are an author. Yes.

Autumn's Here

Parody of
James Whitcomb Riley

From *The Spectator*,
in *The Blue Pencil Review*
(a supplement), Mississippi
State College for Women,
November 28, 1925

Oh, the autumn of the year has come
—there's color everywhere!
There's a dusky, husky, musky,
smoky smelling in the air! And the
leaves are dancing gaily—
they don't give the world a care
Autumn's here!

What fellow said the autumn of the
year was always sad? How could the
whirling, dancing
leaves so gay be aught but glad?
And the man who can't rejoice in
their rejoicing must be bad—
Autumn's here!

Oh, the summer days have ended, and
the autumn has begun,
And the yellow, mellow pumpkins
slowly ripen in the sun,
And the fodder's in the shock, now
the harvest's almost done,
Autumn's here!

Yes, the autumn of the year has
Come—there's color everywhere!
There's a dusky, husky, musky,
smoky smelling in the air! And the
leaves are dancing gaily—
they don't give the world a care,
Autumn's here!

Mosquito

Cover for sheet music composed and published by Eudora's high school teacher, Flo Field Hampton, Summer, 1926

Suggested Illustrations for the Classics

From *The Spectator,* Mississippi State College for Women, November 28, 1925

On Legislative Funding

Welty's first political cartoon, from *The Spectator,* Mississippi State College for Women, February 20, 1926

Have You Registered?

Cartoon captions in rings:

Have you registered?
Have you a box yet?
Well when are you going to matriculate?
Buy your *Meh Lady* while you have the $5.
Who are you?
Do you know Jimmie Goo?
Oh Yes! Who made you come up here?
The way to the hospital is up there & then down there and across yonder.
I'm so glad to meet you.
My name is XXXX.
Oh, where do you room?
Well, well!!
Oh you ought to take that—the grandest sop.

From *The Spectator,* Mississippi State College for Women, October 2, 1926

The Gnat

Parody of a Broadway play entitled *The Bat,* from *The Spectator,* Mississippi State College for Women, October 2, 1926

(The audience is requested not to divulge the outcome of the play to future audiences, as it is a secret.)

Scene: The Library
Time: Closing

ACT I

(Miss Culbertson is stacking up the money from overdue books and at the same time keeping one eye on the library clock to see what it will do next. Suddenly it is midnight. Miss Culbertson is engrossed in counting up the day's spoils when the Gnat enters. He is right scary looking, especially around the feelers.)

The Gnat—"Beulah Culbertson, I have come for that jake."

Miss C.—Silence.

The Gnat—"How come? It is after 9:30." (He wiggles his feelers and shows his fangs. He has fangs. Miss Culbertson is stung.)

Miss C—"Take the money if you must, you insect, but leave me my reading cards."

The Gnat—"I leave nothing." (Exit.)

Miss C.—"Mr. Walker! Mr. Walker!"

(Curtain lowered for two hours to denote lapse of time).

Miss C.—"Oh, Mr. Walker."

(Enter Mr. Walker.)

Mr. Walker—"What!"

Miss C.—"The Gnat has been here and gone. He took the M.S.C.W. library's money."

Mr. Walker—"Now, now. I wonder who that there Gnat is."

(The curtain goes down with everybody wondering.)

ACT II

Scene—Same as Act I, only more people are on the stage. They are wondering, too.

Miss Alexander—"I wonder who the Gnat is? I bet it is Mrs. Galloway."

Miss Holly—"No it isn't."

Dr. Fant—"How come you know so much?"

Miss Holly—"Instinct."

Irene—"I know good and well I ain't no Gnat."

Mrs. Sykes—"Lookit; There goes the Gnat across the skylight!"

Dr. Fant—"We have no skylight, Lydia. However, I firmly believe that if each student would pledge herself to earn four dollars—"

(Mrs. Sykes is foiled.)

Mr. Blair—"Say, what about that man Duff? If he ain't the Gnat he's in cahoots with him."

Claretta—"Maybe he done went down that secret passage."

Dr. Fant—"What secret passage?"

Claretta—"I don't know. Some Junior done tole me about it. She say she believe it leads to de laundry."

Miss Holly—"I knew of a case once where a secret passage led to a cellar. There was wine in the cellar."

Mr. Blair (who all the time has been a detective in disguise)—"Believe it or not, but the college is burning. And don't move, if you value your lives. The Gnat has started the fire to draw you away from the library. He will be back in a moment for Cheyney's *Short History of England*, which he left behind before."

Miss Pohl—"Well, I have to go to fire drill." (Exit.)

Dr. Fant—"Maybe SHE'S the Gnat." (Murmurs.)

(Enter the Gnat.)

Miss Holly—"No, that isn't Miss Pohl. But that Gnat-thing she's wearing does look like a gym suit."

(All jump at Gnat and get him down and step on him. They take off his mask and find he is gone.)

Dr. Fant—"My, my; There's one way out. One of us has to be the Gnat. I shall count out. (He counts out, "Acka Backer Soda Cracker" and Mrs. Sykes is it.)

All—"Well, well, well, well."

(Curtain.)

"I" for Iris—Irma, Imogene

A recollection by Eudora of one of her visits to see her grandfather Jefferson Welty in Hocking County, Ohio; from *The Spectator,* Mississippi State College for Women, November 26, 1926

It was while I was sitting helplessly at the table during one of those inevitable Ohio Sunday dinners, wherein meat, bread, potatoes and kinfolks make a prime struggle for supremacy, that one of the last named made the fatal suggestion. Wouldn't it be nice if I should go to see the new neighbor! She was an artist, they said significantly, and paused. It is generally believed among my relatives that I have an artistic temperament, although they go by only the first two syllables. The artist had just bought the Laning Place and was all by herself; wouldn't it be NICE if I should go to see her.

Tuesday morning I decided I might as well go on, and so I did, not meaning at all to build up illusions on the way. But then the way had margins of apple trees, and the wind was good, and I began to like the way her house looked, up the road—just as though it had been cut out with shiny scissors from very clean white paper and pasted in pieces against the apple trees. The apple trees themselves would have pleased Arthur Rackham with their gray twistiness. I wondered if she had come because of them. I rather hoped she had.

Her house had a card on the door—a large square card with her name in very black letters—"I. Smith." This was interesting: people who used initials for their first names were always either very ashamed of them or were professional enough to be nonchalant. And I reasoned that she must be the latter kind, because if she were going to be ashamed of her name, she would have initialed the Smith.

I knocked on the door, and a voice said "Come in." As soon as I heard it, I knew she had not come to draw the trees; her name was probably Iris and she painted sweet peas on china teacups. I was sorry about it, but I went in. Her studio was empty—the same voice told me to wait and make myself at home. There weren't any teacups lying about, but neither was anything else; she had not finished moving things in yet, of course. Suddenly I saw a bottle of ink: suppose she were named Irma and did banana plants; her voice might be accounted for by describing it as ironic. I was quite absorbed in giving her heavy pen strokes and shell-rimmed glasses when the door shut behind me. I. Smith had come in the room.

In ten minutes I knew all. She had two gold teeth and a ready smile; she was just terribly sorry she had kept me waiting; she did the coat-suit page for Peter's Latest Fashions for Ladies and Young Women—at Cincinnati, my dear—and her name was Imogene Smith. Of course, I did not say anything, but it really would not have mattered in the least to me if she spelled it Smythe—and my dear, wasn't this the deadest place in Ohio.

I think I might just as well claim my artistic temperament.

The Fairy Crepe

Parody of the fairytale genre, with illustration, from *The Spectator,* Mississippi State College for Women, 1927

The Fairy Queen was in a rage
And in a sad, sad plight—
None of her thousand frocks would do
To wear to the ball that night.

Of course, now, she was hard to please,
But what was one to do?
The Queen, like other women-folk,
Must needs have something "new."

Rich merchants brought her splendid cloth,
All bright with magic sheen;
But nothing they could show to her
Would suit the Fairy Queen.

The silk-worms worked in double shifts,
The spiders spun like mad.
But all in vain. The Queen refused
Quite everything they had.

"I'm tired of red-rose velvet gowns,
And wild-rose silk is old.
I will not wear that lacy fern
Or crocus cloth-of-gold."

She wept great tears like diamond dew,
And shook with royal woe
And swore, "Unless I find a frock,
I don't intend to go."

Now that would never do at all,
It would not please the King.
A worried shiver shimmered down
Each Fairy lady's wing.

But then into the Palace pranced
A tiny Fairy pair
Who bore a shining silver chest
With very gentle care.

They bowed before the Fairy Queen
And then began to sing,
"We've brought to you some Fairy Crepe,
The very latest thing!"

They opened up the silver chest.
"Oh," cried the Fairy Queen,
"It is the finest Fairy cloth
I'm sure I've ever seen!"

With merry murmurs, tinkling low,
The court agreed with her.
"Such blushy, crinkled, tissue-cloth,
As light as gossamer!"

She then dried up her diamond tears
And gave a happy whirl—
And paid the Fairy Merchants both
With many a magic pearl.

The Queen wore to the ball that night,
Or so 'twas told to me,
A charming model,—striking, new,
Of crepe from a Myrtle tree!

Staff

Illustration for the masthead page of *Oh, Lady,* a humor magazine founded in 1927 by Eudora and classmates at Mississippi State College for Women

The Garden of Eden

From *Oh, Lady,* Mississippi State College for Women, April 1927

Desire

From *The Spectator,* Mississippi State College for Women, October 23, 1926. During her sophomore year at Mississippi State College for Women, Eudora contributed four serious poems to *The Spectator,* and after her transfer to the University of Wisconsin, one poem to the *Wisconsin Literary Magazine.* This was the end of her poetry career.

I have found a purple flower in a far away place
And I wish that my hair were like swift night clouds
So that I could wear the flower with the proper grace—
No use—

And I know a purple flower would surely come to hate
My saintly silver vase—
So I crush my purple flower on the back door step,
And bury all the leaves beneath the neat back gate,
And I tear the stem in stringy pieces all so nicely brittle
And go inside and polish up my saintly silver vase—
And laugh a little—
(Would you like to see the stain upon the back door step?)

I Could Show You the Colors

From *The Spectator,* in *The Blue Pencil Review* (a literary supplement), Mississippi State College for Women, November 27, 1926

I could show you
    the colors
    in the scarf of
    dreams that I
        would wear
If I were not I—
If I had a star
    to play with, I
    should not mind
    if you held it
    for a little while
    in your hands.
I could talk to you of fairies.

Incident

From *The Spectator,*
Mississippi State College for
Women, May 3, 1927

I found a bright and, curious key,
Made of twisted silver—
It hung on a nail in the highest tree
In the forest of dreams.

I took it down with eager hands—
Thought it beautiful;
Fairies twist the keys of silver
In the forest of dreams.

Through a night of stars did I try the key,
Tried it unceasingly,
But never a tree-door its magic unlocked
In the forest of dreams.

Prophecy

From *The Spectator,* Mississippi State College for Women, May 3, 1927

When I shall have attained, the age of thirty years
And grown accustomed, to the medium things of life
And refrained, from the nightly practice of
Wishing on the first star
And other trivial pastimes.

I shall have a house of my own,
With among other things, a mirror by the bed.
And, every night, after I have said my prayers,
(I shall probably be praying by then)
I shall look long into my own eyes and say,
"You funny person! You knew all the time that it
would be like this,
And yet you went right ahead believing in
fairies."
And, then I shall close my eyes, and
Smile faintly, and begin counting sheep.

You know, I have a deep black hiding-place
More like a witch's pot than anything;
And in the deepest, blackest part I keep
My opals made of dreams and pagan prayers.
And some of them I let you see,
on nights
when the clouded moon flies high,
and makes the fires

That swim with my opal's magic fires.
But I have pearls inside a silver chest;

Pearls like stars when all their shooting lights
Have died, and left calm loveliness
and hopelessness. And when the moon has set
I watch them all alone—all through the night

Shadows

From *Wisconsin Literary Magazine,* April 1928

Even candle-snuffers rust—(snared in candle-smoke)
Inevitably—
Irretrievably—
Shadows are smeared into laughter,
Mountains die,
Dreams are smothered in their sleep,
And beauty goes out with the wind
Through the cracks in the night.

Vacations Lure Jacksonians

From *Jackson Daily News*, June 15, 1930. In the summer of 1930, Eudora contributed feature columns for the *Daily News*.

Large One Underway Soon
Papa Hardest Hit
Suggestion Made That Everyone Start at Once, Make One Huge Party

Vacation time officially begins when junior receives his report card, and officially ends the day before the fish are going to start biting, the day after Sister has at last met a Notre Dame man, and the very day Mamma gives out of stamps.

Just what a vacation really is hard to define.

It is variously known as "a big lie, that's what," "just a nice rest," "the real McCoy, dearie," and "a hallucination."

To most people, however, the vacation is accepted with all its necessary insecticide, Indian bead-work, salt-water taffy, convention delegate ribbons, sea-sickness, and relatives, as is, and is called simply "vacation," though with a smile.

Are Very Necessary

The vacation is a necessary part of our civilization. Without it, the *Literary Digest* these days would be as thin as a lath, and the conversation during September and October would amount to practically nothing.

And where would people put all the ointment?

So it is a very good thing we have vacations.

When we wonder about the origin of the vacation we are not stuck very long. The first one was undoubtedly when Adam and Eve thought it would be nice to get away from the grind awhile and find a nice mosquito-infested place where the rent was higher and there would be a lot more Israelites around.

In the days of the cave man, the vacation was extremely simple. Only the men went on them. No man is going to drag a woman 40 miles.

Of course the simple cave man could not say a complicated word like "vacation." He called it "Koko" or "Phew-phew" instead of "Boop poop pah doop," but all the same he managed to get away from the grind.

Jerking a few of his wife's bangs, he would say, along about June, "Well, pet, I'm off tomorrow on my Koko. You can fix that towel rack in the bathroom while I'm away. Don't follow me. And have some sandwiches ready when I get back."

And that was that.

The cave man would lope off into the muddy wilderness, humming and all his little wife would ever hear from him would be a dried fish.

It seems that the ancients sent dried fish in the spirit in which we send our present advanced colored postals, the sentiment being the same: "Having a wonderful time. Wish you were here, nit."

Sometimes while trekking softly through the wilderness, happy as a lark, our cave man would spy creeping also through the mud another cave man, also on his vacation.

The cry with which two cave men thus similarly bent upon vacations hailed each other was a deep significant "Yo Ho!"

And at night, sitting and rocking in the trees, before time

to go to sleep, these vacationists would exchange confidences about life at home.

While the mosquitoes buzzed dreamily about, as though the scene were not a wilderness but the front porch of a summer hotel, the men would compare wives, make complaints.

"Yeh, but you ought to see the woman I picked out. Good night, the noise and fuss that girl makes just dragging in the wood at night. And late. Always late. And then when I ask her a civil question she only sulks. Women."

The discussion becomes general. Our cave man has a wonderful time while he is away, and along about September he turns up at home asking everybody to look how long such and such a fish was and bragging about sleeping under two blankets the whole darn time.

Following evolution, Papa stays home for the summer and fixes the towel rack in the bathroom while Mamma and the kiddies go to Artichoke Beach on the vacation. Papa doesn't even get a dried fish out of it.

And nowadays the only men who ever say "Yo Ho!" are the Happy Bakers of Wonder Bread, and they never seem to take a vacation either.

There is hardly anyone today who can not say that he has not at some time taken Junior to Chicago to hear Al Capone, or at least Al Capone's gat, and returned with eight woven wash clothes from The Stevens.

In this day and time one is practically required to go to Yellowstone and fry an egg in a geyser.

And—Oh the Places

One can go to Glacier Park and dance with spurs on, one may go up Pike's Peak and send a wire, one may go to New York and read a complete *New York Times*, one may go to California and see how they really make pictures of those awful storms in the movies, with miniature boats, would you ever guess it!

One may go to the National Convention and wear a white satin badge in one's lapel in an expensive hotel lobby and talk back to Room Service. One may take an airplane excursion over Niagara Falls and find what the postcard men have suspected since 1880: How Niagara Looks From the Air.

One may spend a night in a Navajo Desert, a tourist camp, a Zion City jail, Tia Juana, Mexico, a New York sub-let apartment, or a leanto in the Everglades. It's all in a vacation.

And in the extent of the development in modern vacation methods, there seems little left to look forward to in the way of improvement.

Still, there are one or two suggestions which may prove food for some inventor's thoughts.

For instance, somebody like Sinnett ought to invent a home crystal which can be in a breakfast nook or somewhere, which the family must consult before departing on a vacation tour.

This crystal will inform Mamma that at Artichoke Beach everybody plays bridge with octagonal shaped cards, and will even suggest a touch of hay-fever by a cloudy wave of a white handkerchief with the crystal depths.

Sister will look into the future and see that there will

indeed be four Notre Dame boys at Artichoke Beach but that simultaneously she will alas have poison ivy.

Junior will learn of the requirement of the Artichoke Beach Management that all young gentlemen, like their elders, must wear a coat in to dinner.

Father, if he goes, that is, if the family is driving up, will learn that the speedometer of the car will get out of commission a mile out of Tutwiler, Miss., thus dampening all hopes of much future conversation.

Thus the family will stay home for the summer.

All Could Start At Once

A handy device which might be adopted by the United States is this. Make a law that everybody in the country must start out on his vacation trip at the same time.

Think of the spectacle! Four abreast, fender to fender, bumper to bumper, the automobiles will parade along the nation's highways, just like one big family. Somebody in every line will be bound to have a portable radio.

Think of the community spirit that will spring up during this type of vacation! Church services, amateur vaudeville acts, prohibition arguments, bridge games, etc. would all take place just as though this were home instead of the most wonderful vacation yet.

And then—and then, after these weeks of fellowship and real education, the real feature of the vacation would occur when the lines of cars all met. Imagine!

Flowers Talk in Languages of All Races

From *Jackson Daily News,* 1930, undated clipping

Commercialization Takes Little Romance From Nature's Beauties

Just being here, with brides, graduates and the season's allotment of young dreams, the flower rush is on.

"Say it with flowers" is a dictum at first frowned upon by those men [omission] were not of few words, but now accepted; and everybody is saying and hearing things by means of gladioli.

Florist shops have evolved from backyards owned by old maids into marble halls with fountains, canaries and refrigerators.

Car loads of carnations, for instance, come to Jackson all the way from Denver in order that little Mamie may be quite frankly told that papa and mama are proud she is graduating.

Ferns Gain Dignity

The old lady who used to go around to flower shops and beg for sprigs of ferns to stick in her straw fan for church meeting is now told in a business-like way that ferns are shipped here from Florida, Washington and Massachusetts and are no longer onery [sic] but are counted off just like all the big flowers.

Instead of listening to long accounts of operations we are now able, through the language of flowers, to send the question "How is your appendix?" and be glad there is, as yet, no floral reply possible.

With flowers we express joy and best wishes for the bride,

congratulations for the old man on his birthday, sorrow for the bereaved person, and general approval of individuals.

Such generalities in the floral language may be improved and developed in time, until we shall be able to speak with certain modifications, and still not have to say beans with lip or pen. Perhaps the present high divorce rate is due in part to the unqualified statement of a ten-dollar orchid.

But such development will not bring a language to us that is new. There has always been a language of significance of flowers.

Lillie bloomed on Easter, says the Bible.

In the old fairy and folk tales, golden flowers, like golden skeins and hinds and hair, were the illusions that led prince and simpleton through black forests and up glass mountains.

All Have Meanings

Flowers from Chaucer's "white and red" ones, from Milton's blasted one, up through Wordsworth's "meanest flower that blows" to Marcel Proust's cattelya, have had their meanings.

But it took the nineteenth century to put "the language and sentiment of flowers" directly into the etiquette book.

Along with the oraculum, sample love letters, household receipts, the dictionary rhymes, the method of observing wedding anniversaries, elementary gymnastics, conundrums, and choice selections from the best authors, a complete list of the meaning of flowers was necessary to make the book adequate.

We find in this list a Colchicum or Meadow Saffron means "My best days are past." A cowslip betokens "Pensiveness and Winning Grace." To express "Love at First Sight" all you need to send the party is acoeoposis Arkansa. On the other hand, "Could you bear poverty?" may be asked with a Browallia, whatever that is.

Girls, a gift of roses is not in itself thrilling. Be sure as to what kind of rose you have received. A Carolina rose means simply, "Love is Dangerous," while a Christmas rose means "Tranquilize Thy Anxiety" and a Damask rose means "Brilliant Complexion." A single rose says "Simplicity." A single rose declares "Call me not Beautiful," a Japan rose means "Beauty is your Only Attraction," and a Maiden Blush rose means "If you love me, you will find it out." A popular reply flower was undoubtedly the Coltsfoot, which said "Justices shall be done."

But undoubtedly the pride of the flower language lay in the bouquet. A very interesting correspondence was possible with just a little care and dexterity. For instance, if you wanted to say "May maternal love protect your truth in innocence and joy" all you needed was some moss, some bearded crepis, a few primroses, a daisy and a hand full of wood sorrel.

A natty little rebuke was made possible by some London Pride, a Lobelia, and some Laburnum. Thus you have said "Your frivolity and malevolence will cause you to be forsaken by all." And "let the bonds of marriage unite us" was simply and feelingly expressed by a Blue Convovulus, a piece of ivy and a few whole straws.

The expression of flowers is varied by changing their positions. "Place a marigold on the head," says the etiquette book, "and it signifies "mental anguish;" on the bosom, "indifference."

When a flower is given, the pronoun "I" is understood by bending it to the right; "thou" by inclining it to the left. "Yes" is implied by kissing the flower.

Meaning Modified

When the petals are one by one pinched off and cast away, the general idea thus carried across is "no." "I offer you" is expressed by a leaf of the Virginia Creeper.

Remember, all this was before the days when people would say anything and everything on a card. There was a little interest in getting flowers in the old days, evidently. In the first place you got strange ones, bearded crepis or corn cockle, which challenged your wits for a minute or two. In the second place, you could answer anonymously after a little rummaging in your backyard, disguised under a sun hat.

The flower custom in the nineteenth century started out to be a contest. Now it remains only a commercialized custom—beautiful none the less, of course, but the really coy feature of it, the repartee between the sexes, has been thrown over to other pursuits like the straw vote polling on prohibition.

The Editor's Mike

From *Lamar Life Radio News,* December 27, 1931–January 2, 1932. In 1931–32 Eudora worked as editor of the newsletter for WJDX, the Jackson radio station established by her father.

This being the New Year edition of the *Radio News,* we should declare anew our persistent aim to please our radio public. And indeed it's the truth—we do try to please all of the people all of the time, which Aesop or somebody in the second reader said was nigh impossible. We keep telling you that "this is your radio station" and we mean it. However, there are two ways of interpreting that remark "this is your radio station." You can take it personally or democratically.

The air belongs to everyone—even the people who haven't got radio sets. But all the people who have radio sets have a say-so about what goes on the air. We don't mean their personal say-so. We mean rather a lump say-so. We haven't signed up Gene and Glenn, for instance, because an old lady with spectacles, lavender perfume, and a spidery handwriting from Picayune, Miss., if there is such a person, asked us to. We are putting Gene and Glenn back on the air because at least two thirds of our radio audience has indicated its desolation without Gene and Glenn. We got the chance to return them to you and we are doing it, because "this is your radio station." But if one person takes that remark personally and doesn't like Gene and Glenn and writes us to remove them instantly, we won't do it. This would be an example of terrible misunderstanding.

It is one of the fruits of democracy that you get over the air what the majority likes to hear. The number of radios in the United States is enormous. And the sum total of all the families and neighbors who listen to those sets comprise the object of that declaration "This is your radio station."

Adaptation of your personal desires and preferences to

those of society at large is the major problem of living anyway; and each person with a radio set must content himself with realizing that in order to make a radio station "your radio station," the preferences of the audience at large are considered first.

So in the New Year, we are indeed anxious to make your radio station measure up to what you all want. Your fan mail will help. Your complaints won't because it's in only a positive way that your letters have influence. Not enough people complain to carry any weight against the number of people who praise. So write in with praise for what you like, and the effects will be forthcoming. The more letters we have, a greater representation of the preferences of the audience at large will be available to the station so that programs to please the most of you can be arranged. And the human race is so constituted that what pleases the most of you pleases you, Mr. A., and you, Mrs. B, and you, Miss C.

It is most pleasant to try to give our audience what it wants—WJDX's audience is one of the most responsive and appreciative of all station audiences; that's proven statistically by our files of letters and known up at NBC. You are very nice. We just want to explain why we can't do any more for you than we are doing. We have to please all of the people all of the time. That's a pretty big job.

The Editor's Mike

From *Lamar Life Radio News,* May 29–June 4, 1932

When the Derby at Epsom Downs, England, was first run in 1780, little did the be-wigged gentlemen who attended guess that in two centuries and a half, at 7:45 on a June morning, we should be hearing from the Downs its hundred and fifty-second sequel. However, it's all matter of fact in our civilization; and Tommy and Betty will hear the Derby at breakfast June first and think the fact no more remarkable than that their Puffed Wheat has been exploded eight times. Which may be the correct attitude. Our civilization thrusts many wonders upon us, and we can accept them all with the most condescending notice, and they continue to be brought out of inventors' closets and thrust upon us.

However, there is something unusual in a horse race described in an accent that wears a monocle, at the engaging hour of seven thirty in the morning, when it isn't even running until afternoon. We can't help but feel how far is the point we have now reached in "progress." Where an international broadcast of a concert would move us only to polite admiration of what radio can do, the Epsom Derby at breakfast time works us up to the point of excitement. The radio IS a wonderful invention. We ARE living in fast times, no doubt about it. When a sudden sound in your ear makes you see a cloud of Epsom Downs dust rise before your eyes as the race is on, you know that the radio is wonderful. In spite of previous evidence of triumph over the ether it takes a horse race to make the wonder graphic for us.

The Editor's Mike

From *Lamar Life Radio News*, September 11–17, 1932

Cheerio! The editor is back at the microphone, good people, a bit out of breath, but back. Claudia Brewer is at this very minute getting a brilliant smile of gratitude from us for the noble work she did on the news for the past three issues, and from now on the paper is going to be up to that standard or break the presses. Couldn't you tell we were jaded the few weeks before we left? But now that we've had a vacation we have a beautifully fresh mind, almost capable of the juggling we're going to do for you on page 3 next week.

They're retrenching on Daylight Saving Time up there at the network headquarters, and that means we'll all move up an hour down here by the time the next issue comes out. If you're a Morning Devotions fan, you can stay in bed an hour longer now. But don't worry yet. We're the one that has to worry, we are so bad in arithmetic and this thing means adding one to every hour of the day. Just try to get a clear fresh mind this week and next week you can be ready for the schedule.

As for being out of breath, as we are, that's due to wonder. Wonder at the sizes of things. We saw the NBC studios in New York, which were so very big, and we saw Paul Whiteman, who has contracted into maestro proportions. It got us all mixed up. Studios are supposed to be nice and compact, we thought, and Paul Whiteman is supposed to be capable of filling space from here to New York. It's all just backwards. Paul is really down to almost nothing, folks—he is so slim and sprightly you begin to notice almost instantly he has a big mustache. We think he's heading for the athletic type. The silent muscle, etc. And the studios are so drafty—really too big, it seemed to us. Our orchestra could all get in one of them and play trombones within a radius of a good many centimeters with their feet up and a *very* large audience could come in and watch.

What's so wonderful about that, though? There's no place like home. WJDX is really just like NBC on a small scale—the only thing we lack is a retinue of blonde hostesses, although we have our own Lois McCormick. So what the heck?

Whose Photo Do You Want to See Next?

From *Lamar Life Radio News*, September 11–17, 1932

While we were gone a picture of Ralph Maddox got in the *Radio News*. The editor had been holding out on this picture until Ralph quit taking her rightful parking places on Capitol Street, but the idea was futile. He cared naught for publicity. Now all we can do is mark up the picture with a pair of goggles, curly hair, and a handlebar moustache. However, the public response to the printing of the picture was so great that we may have to run it again some time. Many people were surprised at the youthful appearance of Ralph, whose voice denotes such assurance and judicial conviction. Ralph is really old for his years and quite pleasant, his only fault being parking in the only place left on Capitol Street when we want it.

Please write in and tell us whose pictures you'd like to see and we'll do our best to get them for you. This paper is to please, you know. Write your letter to the Editor, WJDX.

Big Flood Drama in the Studio

From *Lamar Life Radio News,* January 24–30, 1932

Flood times came to WJDX not long ago with a tide of water right through the studio. When the eleventh floor of a Jackson skyscraper floods, you know it. When Mrs. Foster, genial secretary, etc., came to work that morning she couldn't get the door open. She pushed and pushed and something pushed back. "Ah-ah, Mr. Coullet!" she called, thinking the maestro was playing tricks. But no sound came but the bubbling of water. When she got the door open, Mrs. Foster was amazed to see that the studio was resting, a little uneasily, on a floating carpet. It was like a romantic swamp scene, with the desk in a sodden mass holding down one end of the rug and dismal dripping musical instruments huddled together in the back room. All the windows and doors had been closed the night before but still there was the flood. Seepage it was—from the flagpole. The torrents of rain that had flooded Jackson that morning had come in good portion to rest on the Lamar roof, and then, having nothing better to do, went on in to the studio. Mr. Harris wore long shiny magnificent arctics for several days after that morning. The rugs are being dried and the three inches of water from under them were cordially cussed and sent to the basement in dirty buckets. We hope that's a lesson. The damage was not great, only a box of fox trots being thoroughly soaked, fading the blues and dampening the hot numbers, and the control mechanism and musical instruments being snatched from the waters in time. But don't think that if you live on the eleventh floor you can't have a flood. Anything can happen in a radio station.

Jackson Composer Has Full Year Program

From *Jackson State Tribune,* June 19, 1933. In 1933, Eudora wrote for the *Jackson State Tribune,* a short-lived newspaper founded by her friend Ralph Hilton.

K-14, the Pullman that brings most Jackson adventurers home to brood, doesn't mean a thing to A. Lehman Engel, because he's going back in the fall. A. Lehman Engel, on the other hand, probably means a lot to K-14, because he's famous—and K-14 may well expect to make the Jackson trip some day dressed to kill, as well as a Pullman car can be, in a lot of bunting with a slew of roses around lower 9, from the window of which Mr. Engel may be expected to look with his pleasing modesty and affecting devotion upon Jackson, the place of his birth.

Not that the decorations would have to wait—Mr. Engel has enough press notices, if he would get them together, to decorate a booth at a fair, with enough let over for leis for the coffee gins, but the future tantalizes with "Just wait—there'll be more and more." There are plans for next year which include items like this:

A new piece of music of a satiric nature for Martha Graham, the dancer; a lecture tour with Henry Compson, the pianist, in a program of contemporary American music; a new revue for which he will write and direct the music; performances of his compositions at the Festival of American Music in New York, the Yaddo Festival of American Music at Saratoga Springs, the California Society of Contemporary Music at San Francisco, the concerts of Dr. Hans Pless in Vienna, and a New York broadcasting studio and a leading national phonograph company. Perhaps the news most glamorous to the ear is that Madame Catharine Reiner of the Budapest Opera is to sing some of his songs in New York recitals. What a contact—a Jacksonian with Budapest! The whole town could go cosmopolitan on less than that, if it wanted to.

Recognized

Elected in 1933 to the Pan-American Association of Composers, in which there are only thirty members in both the Americas, so far; as one of the eight in the Young Composers Group organized by Aaron Copland; his name affixed as one of the founders of the Composers Protective Association recently reported in the *New York Times*, Mr. Engel has achieved definite important recognition in other ways besides the significant applause of those who know contemporary music and the favorable criticism of his various undertakings in the newspapers and music journals. It is with considerable interest therefore that we find he has something to say especially to Jackson and her music clubs.

Preoccupied as he is with American music and its prospects for significant existence, Mr. Engel thinks it highly important that music clubs in every community be impressed with certain facts which he and most contemporary composers are working with.

"In music clubs everywhere in the country," said Mr. Engel, "choice of materials is limited to one class of music invariably out of date and never, even in its heyday, a fine artistic type. While I like Charles Cadman personally and am sorry that he belonged to a period in American music which even he realizes was not of a very high type, I cannot console him nor his followers by denying that their output was of no intrinsic value. Least of all was it American; for it was a very technically deficient and cheap imitation of something which was already exhausted by European composers.

"I propose on the other hand that our music clubs make an effort to understand the works of men who are original, American and contemporary; and I suggest people like Roy Harris, Aaron Copland, Roger Sessions, and the like. In the east these men are known and their works extensively performed; and around them there has grown up a literature by such eminent critics as Paul Rosenfeld, Henry Cowell, and John Tasker Howard.

"The music clubs in the smaller places and the places far removed from music centers are of great importance to the growth and assimilation of American music. They can be of immense value if they will perform more important and contemporary works, and if they will attempt to understand the performances through frequent repetition and detailed study, making of the club an educational rather than a superficial or social group.

"We do have an American music—and it is up to the people to keep it alive; to do that, they must first discover it.

"To gain a knowledge and understanding of anything that is new and that is fine," Mr. Engel added, "may mean putting oneself to a good deal of trouble to make it accessible. Compositions by people like Oley Speaks, Lily Strickland, Amy Woodforde-Finden, Carrie Jacobs-Bond, and Ethelbert Nevin may be ever so charming when heard over a luncheon table, but have never been and never will be of any intrinsic importance. To listen intelligently to a Roy Harris sonata requires no more (and in fact no less) attention than is required of a Beethoven sonata. Each is worthy of the energy required in one's full appreciation, and there is no approach to either without full mental and spiritual participation."

Mr. Engel gives a practical message in this and knows whereof he speaks. He has traveled in many fields, perhaps the most Elysian being that where Martha Graham, the Dance Centre, Jacques Charrier, and Harry Losee are dancing to his music. Starting out with an opera, "Pierrot of the Minute," which he wrote while studying in Cincinnati in 1925, he has successfully proceeded to conduct chorales, appear in recitals of his compositions, contribute to music journals, deliver lectures, compose songs, choruses, dance cycles, and another opera, "Job," direct music for the Little Temple, a newly formed and exclusive religious organization in New York, direct a radio series over WEVD on contemporary American music, and participate in an assortment of other activities bewildering in number but all integrated by the direct intent of a dominant talent.

About "Rain"

He has had his work performed by important artists and received with considerable praise. About "Rain," a song written in 1932 and published by Chester, Ltd., London, *Musical America* for February says: "For unaccompanied mixed voices we have a brief piece called "Rain" by A. Lehman Engel. It is his Opus 1, and is one of the most amazing part songs that has come our way. Mr. Engel has a gift that is unusually expressive. He is a young composer, in his twenties, is breaking paths, and shows the influence of the modern Germans who write for chorus. But he also makes us feel that he has something to say and the courage to say it his way. In that direction lies hope."

"Rain" was since performed by the Dessoff Choirs in Town Hall, New York, where it was well received. An amusing criticism appeared in the *New York Evening Post*:

"'Rain' by A. Lehman Engel, which had its first performance anywhere has a pleasing reminiscent melancholy. It was strongly applauded and from one corner of the hall the applause was a little prolonged. Possibly there was a claque from the Juilliard Graduate School where Mr. Engel is a fellow, and maybe a jolly good fellow."

Mr. Engel, though obviously both jolly and pretty good, denied he heard any claquing noise that night. Incidentally he has just won his fourth fellowship at the Juilliard, an unusual distinction.

"Ceremonials," a large dance cycle composed for four wind instruments, male voices, and piano, was Mr. Engel's first work in association with Martha Graham, who performed it at the Guild Theatre and on tour and is planning to revive it next season. Martha Graham, who very beautifully assumed a Gothic posture in long robes for her latest photohap in *Vanity Fair*, is one of the most unusual of present American dancers. Critics said she reached the high point in her career in the season just ended when she danced "Ekstasis," two fragments composed by Mr. Engel. John Martin, critic of the *New York Times*, says this of the recital:

> "In the new lyric fragments entitled 'Ekstasis,' it reaches its height in an enchantingly lovely suite. For all its tenuous use of design and substance, it is yet warm and rich and eminently unsubstantial. Here indeed, Miss Graham has not only moved into a new field but has also touched a new level of achievement. A. Lehman Engel's music provides it with an admirable web of sound against which to weave its pattern."

In contrast to his music for her, Mr. Engel has composed a series of Indian pieces, the choreography of which is probably to be by Jacques Cartier, and a ballet, "Phobias," recently performed at the Barbizon-Plaza by the New York Dance Centre.

Able Leader

Those of us who attended the recent high school graduation exercises and witnessed Mr. Engel's bright conducting of the "Alma Mater," music he composed at fifteen, will be interested to read in the *New York Times* about his proficiency as shown in the recent conducting of the American premiere of "Der Jasager," an opera by Kurt Weill. "He conducted with vivacity and assurance says the *Times*. "He displayed an unusual gift with baton in hand," said the *Musical Leader* (to flip through the press notices), "his sense of rhythm and dynamic values was unusual for a young director." "Der Jasager" was a daring departure in performance from most opera material and offered unique difficulties, since the singers were chosen from non-professionals and the chorus was a group of children. The opera was quite a choice importation, having been performed successfully hundreds of times abroad; and creditably to undertake it here was a dazzling feather in any conductor's cap. The opera and the conductor were both unanimously acclaimed by a brilliant audience of patrons and critics, including Jascha Heifetz, George Gershwin, Nathaniel Shilkret, Irene Lewisohn, Nicolai Mednikoff, Rubin Goldmark, Vladimir Dukelsky, and many others. This was the climax of Mr. Engel's past season.

Limericks

In 1933 when Frank Lyell, a long-time friend of Eudora's, was enrolled at Princeton University and rode the train from Jackson to Chicago enroute to New Jersey, Eudora offered "a limerick for every stop."

Illustrated letter, Eudora Welty to Frank Lyell, Princeton University, 1933. From the Eudora Welty Collection, Mississippi Department of Archives and History. Used by permission of Louis Lyell

Pickens

There was a young lady of Pickens
Who read Longfellow, Burns, Scott and Dickens
When they said, "You're intense,"
She replied, "No offense,"
But my interest first lags and then quickens."

Durant

There was a young girl of Durant
When they said, "What's the news of your aunt?"
She replied "poop de doo,"
Poop de dee, poop de doo,"
That disinterested girl of Durant.

Winona

There was an old girl of Winona
Who lived in a pongee Kimono—
When the Lion's Club came thru
She politely withdrew,
That delicate gal of Winona.

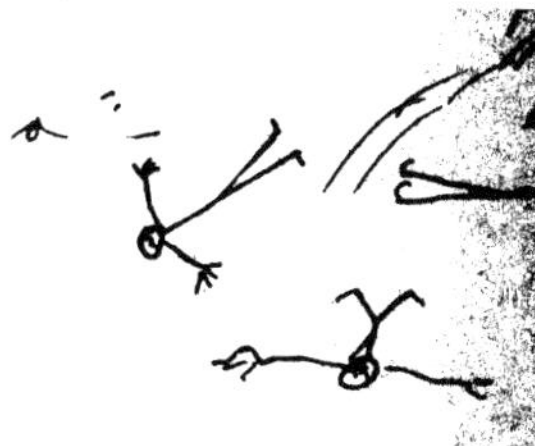

Chattanooga

An old-fashioned girl of Chattanooga
Had an old-fashioned horn that went "ooga."
& with little or no pity
Bumped all in the city
Conditioned to "beep" and not "ooga."

Fulton, Kentucky

There was a young lady of Fulton
But this flower of the South was a-wilton
She would sleep 24
Hours a day if not more,
On a theory that Fulton's a dull town.

Cairo, Illinois

There was a young lady of Cairo
Who purchased a green autogiro
When they said, "You'll come down,"
She replied with a frown,
"But not necessarily in Cairo."

Chicago

There was a young girl of Chicago
Who liked Poet and Peasant—largo.
She said "Ain't it pleasant
To read "Poet and Peasant"—
It renders me utterly ga-ga.

Society Items

From the fall of 1933 to 1935, Eudora wrote Jackson society news items for the Memphis *Commercial Appeal.*

They never were going to let joy be confined here for very long. First the Pi Kappa Alphas, after the local chapter had worked with garnet and gold decorations until the Armory looked like a sweetheart on parade, threw the season open with a until-four-thirty event Wednesday. Mart Brit, who learned in a real nightclub, was here with his Victor recording orchestra, and the [s]ong was kicked around in frenzied tenor by Charles Gramp, who electrified all. Smoothly accomplished and enchanting were the two no-breaks, the two specials, the visitors' lead-out and the Pi Kappa Alpha lead-out. And every dream girl of Pi K. A. looked dreamy in a special rosebud corsage. . . .

Speaking of feathers, no bride has worn them yet, although they all read in *Vogue* that they could do it. However, the next best thing—a maid of honor wore the color chartreuse. Miss Bethany Swearingen, who was Miss Mary Louise Forter's maid of honor when she married Brother Mac, was scintillating in that very color—as far as we know—the first time it's been in a wedding. That is a mark of advance we consider. Miss Swearingen has since returned to Chicago, where she writes very smart advertising copy in—perhaps—chartreuse ink, for business could not be too proletarian with Miss Swearingen in it.

SEPTEMBER 10, 1933

Chollie Knickerjackson tells me that Sallie Beard looked regal in white crepe at the Phi Mu dance Tuesday eve; that Maud McLean wore cordial velvet, which leaves much up to Miss McLean, who, however, was really intoxicating. Margaret Flowers, the new president, shone, we hear further, in white with gardenia corsage. Catherine Jones, who is outgoing clear to Terre Haute, Ind., where she will enter St. Mary of the Woods, still looked sweetly presidential in a flowered frock.

Billy Vick, goes on Chollie, looked like Lynn Fontanne in a deep purple crepe—a salute, Billy. And Winifred Green was the radiant southern beauty in black silk with white collar and a colonial bouquet. Frances McWillie was her true gay self in flowered chiffon, and everybody was glad to see Joe Ellis Love appearing at their dance—wearing beige with the Buie antique jewelry, too. Mrs. Malcolm Smith, Elise Herring to us, dropped in here from St. Louis, looking marvelous.

Lemma Gordon wore red—and would have been brilliant even without brilliants, but the frock had brilliants and Lemma dazzled. Louise Green was vivacious over French flowers on her white organdy frock. Norvelle Beard, who helped arrange the dance, was in a handsome pale blue velvet, and Meredith Owen came in pink with coq feathers, which everyone said was almost a lei. Helen Yerger, who came up from Mounds, La., wore with her lavender crepe a veiled lavender hat, and managed to be far from nostalgic.

Mary Gillespie was over from Raymond in blue beaded crepe. All in black and white organdy with a black and white evening hat and consequently very smart was Indian Sykes. And many another beautiful Phi Mu came deliciously gowned to her dance. . . . Afterwards time and confetti flew until time to go, pleasant dreams. . . .

Miss Lucy Murphy Mallico, ex-queen of the carnival, had

a part Wednesday night. Everyone first swam and then played murder until everyone had been murdered. Cooling drinks were served the guests.

SEPTEMBER 17, 1933

You must consider, you must admit, that it has taken time to produce a complete magnolia tree in bloom, a row of accurately colored azalea bushes, a line of iris, eternally fresh, and a flock of hollyhocks, all snipped, stitched, cut and contrived out of cotton stuffs; not to mention 55 very beautiful girls in the flesh; and transport all, leaf and baggage, 125 miles. Yet that is what the Natchez Garden people have done; and this tableaux they brought to Jackson at the Natchez Garden Ball on Friday evening, showed all the glories of this creation and transportation.

SEPTEMBER 21, 1933

The University Club ran a Who's Who contest Saturday night, when everybody had to come to the dance as his favorite wild animal. A grand prize was awarded for the most "beastly" outfit by the committee, Mr. Jimmy Hewes, Mr. Bernard Tighe, Mr. Tom Crockett, Mr. Marcellus Green and Mr. John Underwood. It was all quite amazing."

OCTOBER 15, 1933

Jackson society is going to get what it has wanted for a long long time—debutantes! The first will be introduced in a waiting society the first week in November under the wing of the University Club. A reception will be the first event when several will make their first bows. Balls, teas, and all manner of gay events will follow, to make the winter the brightest in Jackson's history.

OCTOBER 22, 1933

The high stepping of highbred horses brought the horse show on Thursday to the forefront of Jackson's social interest during the past week. The gleam of cups, the bright dash of autumn frocks, the whole color of track excitement made the afternoon memorable.

Entries from all over the state brought spectators from far and near. Jackson's interest in riding is higher than ever, and the brilliant show of Thursday captured its heart.

OCTOBER 29, 1933

The Carnival Ball next month is anticipated by Jackson society, members of which have little to interest them in January.

This week a spelling bee offered its old-fashioned charms to hundreds of Jacksonians and members of the Legislature and their wives who attended, and did a little spelling Wednesday evening at the Edwards House, for the benefit of the Kings Daughters here. Judge Garland Lyell gave out the words, while Supreme Court Clerk Tom Q. Elli and Sam Purvis, legislator from Union County, were captains of the two teams. They spelled each other down in the fanciest way until young Brewer Sheldon, 12-year-old grandson of former Governor Sheldon of Nebraska, held everyone at bay by spelling "phthistic," which ended the match and rightly so.

The King's Daughters are running a community hospital, to which the funds will go.

JANUARY 14, 1934

The Queen of Love and Beauty is at present a mere pawn in the hands of Dame Rumor, who identifies her as a different young socialite maid every day in the week. However her court is preparing to bear lavish witness to her charms on the evening of the thirteenth when Rex will rule with her on her carnival throne.

OCTOBER 21, 1933

Around the "court" of Louis the Fourteenth, Jackson's Carnival Ball will be constructed. The costumes are already here. The ladies, in brocades, silver and gold, in velvets and silks of the brilliant period will be escorted by courtiers equally grand in silk knee-britches and square-cut coats with lace jabots. All members of the court will appear in wigs.

FEBRUARY 4, 1933

Club women seem to have been the first to contract spring fever; their activity has supplied what news Jackson has had for the week. Garden clubs of the state convened in Pass Christian, and many persons augmented the hegira to the south to see the Mobile Azalea Trail in its glory.

MARCH 25, 1934

The Kappa Sigma barn dance took place on Tuesday night at the Armory. The setting was done to the life, with hay, lanterns, and wagon wheels, and all guests came attired in overalls and the gayest of ginghams.

JUNE 10, 1934

Caricatures

Sent to Frank Lyell at Princeton University, 1933. From The Eudora Welty House Collection, Mississippi Department of Archives and History.

Wm Faulkner

Mae West

Prince of Wales

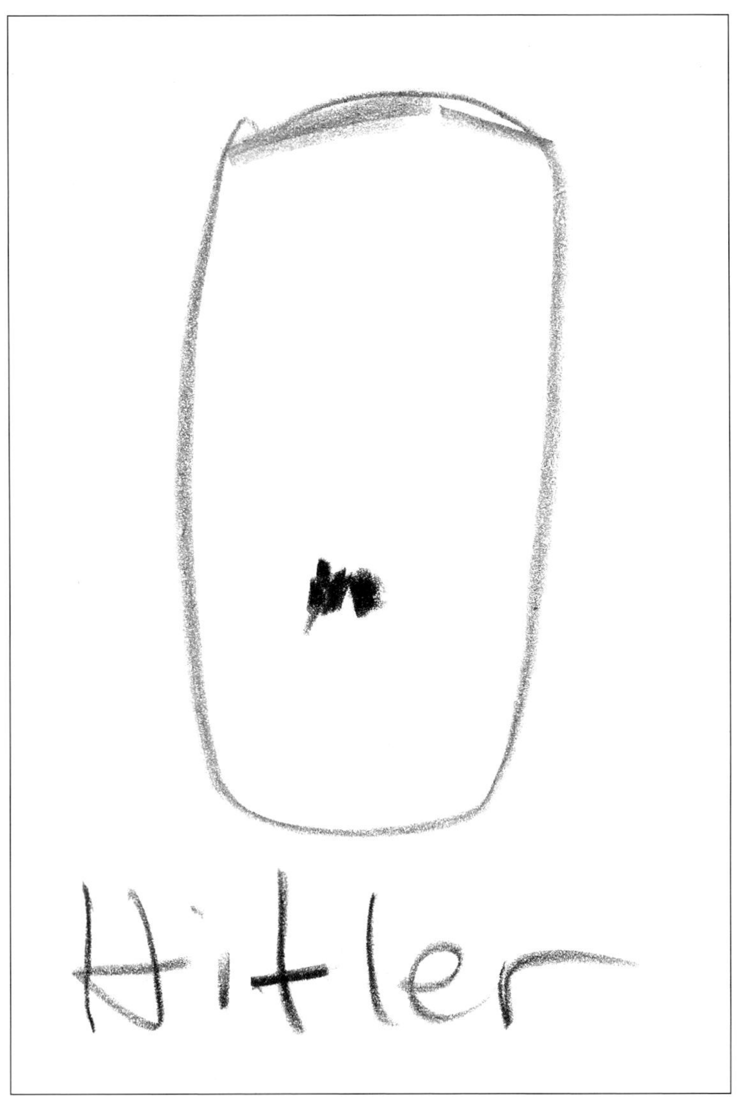
Hitler

The
Shiek
of
Araby

Dorothy Dix

Eudora umpires for brothers Walter and Edward in this staged photograph taken by her father, Christian Welty. She later explained that she was in reality a baseball player.

Eudora strikes a model's pose at the Monument to the Women of the Confederacy on the grounds of Mississippi's New Capitol, late 1920s.

Eudora, probably in her backyard on Pinehurst Street, late 1920s

Eudora, Frank Lyell, Lehman Engel, and other friends often staged comic photographs in the early 1930s. This could be Welty as Groucho Marx, whom she admired, or as a mountain man with his moonshine.

Eudora, in front of her house on Pinehurst Street, early 1930. She is possibly spoofing "The Magic Carpet" fairytale.

Frank Lyell in sombrero and tie serenades Eudora in fringed scarf and shawl as she perches in a tree at Annandelle, early 1930s. The photograph could have been taken by Lehman Engel or Robert Daniel.

In 1937 Eudora, Frank Lyell, and Robert Daniel worked on a book which satirized poetry and was to be called "Lilies That Fester." This photograph, probably taken by Frank Lyell or Robert Daniel, was to be used to advertise the book, which was never published.

Frank Lyell and Eudora pose for a photograph to be used for "Lilies That Fester," ca. 1937.

In this undated photograph, Eudora lounges on railroad tracks, probably those of the Illinois Central line which brought passenger trains through Jackson.